A WORKBOOK FOR

New Testament Syntax

A WORKBOOK FOR

New Testament Syntax

COMPANION TO *BASICS OF NEW TESTAMENT SYNTAX*
AND *GREEK GRAMMAR BEYOND THE BASICS:*
AN EXEGETICAL SYNTAX OF THE NEW TESTAMENT

Daniel B. Wallace
and
Grant G. Edwards

ZONDERVAN.com/
AUTHORTRACKER
follow your favorite authors

ZONDERVAN

A Workbook for New Testament Syntax
Copyright © 2007 by Daniel B. Wallace and Grant G. Edwards

Requests for information should be addressed to:
Zondervan, *Grand Rapids, Michigan 49530*

ISBN 978-0-310-27389-9

Interior design: Mark Sheeres

Printed in the United States of America

23 24 25 26 27 28 29 30 • 25 24 23 22 21 20 19 18 17 16

Table of Contents

Acknowledgments

This workbook has gone through many hands before it went to the press. It is our privilege to acknowledge those who have contributed to it, making it a more usable handmaiden to the learning of Greek syntax.

Professor Jim Blankenship of John Brown University is to be thanked for his many valuable suggestions after working through a rough draft of the *Workbook*. His sixth sense for pedagogical needs has improved this work substantially.

We are also grateful to the many field-testers, including students in Advanced Greek Grammar at Dallas Seminary (spring 2006), as well as students in Honors First-Year Greek (spring 2007). These two groups represent a wide diversity in Greek background, but each gave helpful input on the shape of the *Workbook*.

Dan Wallace's interns for 2006 – 2007 at Dallas Seminary — Steve Hellman, Garrett Mathis, and Brian Wright — have done a great deal of grunt work: proofreading, culling the New Testament for examples, producing diagrams, adding vocabulary, more proofreading. Brian especially is to be singled out; we relied on his keen eye several times in the process of meeting deadlines. Indeed, he came through with flying colors when Dan was in "panic mode"!

Finally, we wish to give our heartiest thanks to our editor, Verlyn Verbrugge. His constant encouragement, patience, wisdom, and knowledge of Greek syntax were all essential ingredients that went into the mix.

Without the input of all these people, this *Workbook* would be immeasurably poorer. Perhaps if we accepted even more of their suggestions, it would be significantly better. But it is what it is because we are what we are: recalcitrant grammarians with thick skins and thicker skulls.

Grant G. Edwards and Daniel B. Wallace

Preface

If the adage is true that practice makes perfect, then an essential component in mastering Greek syntax should be exercises in identifying the syntactical uses.

There are, however, hurdles to overcome in designing a workbook for Greek syntax. The approach to the exercises is more of a challenge than one might think. Syntax, far more than translation or parsing, relies heavily on the context. In order to offer drills in syntax, a sufficient context is necessary. This means that isolated verses, though valuable for a pedagogical book on syntax, have certain inherent deficiencies in a workbook. Consequently, the approach that asks students to translate individual verses and to identify various syntactical uses can never reinforce the more subtle nuances since it does not place those verses in their context.

The alternative is to have students translate through a whole book of the New Testament, identifying syntactical features as they go along. This has the advantage of getting them to work within the context of the book. But it also has inherent disadvantages. For one, the books of the New Testament were not intended to be utilized for syntactical analysis. Thus, many of the common categories of usage will simply not get reinforced. Second, the students get exposure to only one genre, leaving them with an artificial sense of the kinds and amounts of various syntactical features they will see in the New Testament.

A Workbook for New Testament Syntax presents a *tertium quid*: it incorporates the strengths of both of the above approaches, while minimizing the weaknesses. Each lesson is comprised of 15 to 30 verses. These verses are continuous: that is, they are placed in their respective contexts and are prefaced by a brief introduction. Usually two or three "syntax clusters" — or passages that are rich in the particular syntactical categories under examination — are in each lesson. As well, there are some "warm-up" verses that need little context to help the student determine the syntactical usage. All vocabulary words that occur less than fifty times are listed at the beginning of each passage.

The advantages of this approach are that the students see syntax in context, get exposed to various genres and authors, and get practice in the common syntactical categories. Our goal, in fact, has been to include at least one question on each of the major syntactical categories. We believe that this approach will prove to be the least frustrating and most rewarding for the student.

This workbook has been especially designed to work with Daniel B. Wallace's *Basics of New Testament Syntax* (Grand Rapids: Zondervan, 2000; here abbreviated *Basics*) as well as with Wallace's *Greek Grammar beyond the Basics: An Exegetical Syntax of the New Testament* (Zondervan, 1996; here abbreviated *ExSyn*). But it should work well with virtually any intermediate grammar.[1]

There are three different ways to use this *Workbook*. (We are referencing these suggestions to usage with *The Basics of New Testament Syntax*.)

First, in an *ideal* world the student should go through the following steps as he or she learns New Testament Greek grammar:

---

[1] The basic issue will be that the terminology for the syntactical categories differs from grammar to grammar. But this should only cause problems if the teacher intends to use the answer key that we are providing for this workbook. With a few adjustments, even that should cause little difficulty.

1. Read through the section in the *Basics*, memorizing the gist of the arrowed and daggered categories.[2] Also, become somewhat familiar with the rest of the categories.

2. Read the Greek texts in this workbook out loud.

3. Memorize the vocabulary listed below the Greek text (all words occurring less than fifty times in the New Testament) — at least long enough to work through the translation.

4. Translate the passages, at least mentally.

5. Work through the *Workbook*, checking your answers with the descriptions of the usages in *Basics*.

That's in an ideal world. Of course, we are well aware that students tend to find (what they think is) the path of least resistance (we know; we've done it ourselves!). They also succumb to the tyranny of the urgent. What often happens is the *practical route:*

1. Read through the section in the *Basics*, memorizing nothing.

2. Skip the reading of the Greek text out loud.

3. Only glance at the vocabulary list as necessary.

4. Do a rough translation in your mind, but one that is not particularly coherent.

5. Give answers to the workbook questions thirty minutes before the class starts so that *something* can be written down. Fake your way through oral recitation.

But there is a *via media* approach. The professor should encourage students to take the ideal route as much as possible, since it really will save time and increase retention. Nonetheless, this final approach involves some helpful shortcuts:

1. Read through the section in the *Basics*, writing down the keys to identification for the arrowed and daggered categories.

2. Read the Greek texts in the *Workbook* out loud.

3. Open your copy of the Greek New Testament and photocopy the vocabulary lists so that you can consult both as you work through the syntactical questions.

4. Translate the texts, at least mentally.

5. Work through the Workbook, consulting *Basics* as you go.

If the professor requires the ideal method, there are ways in which he or she can test the students to see if they are following it. But in the least, we recommend that the *via media* approach be followed.

---

[2] *Arrowed* categories refer to those usages that are common in the New Testament and should be committed to memory. *Daggered* categories refer to those usages that are overused in exegetical literature.

Introduction

As you complete the exercises in this *Workbook*, there are a few things to keep in mind:

1. The twenty lessons correspond *approximately* to the chapters in Daniel B. Wallace's *Basics of New Testament Syntax* (*Basics*) and *Greek Grammar beyond the Basics: An Exegetical Syntax of the New Testament* (*ExSyn*). But there are no specific lessons on prepositions, conjunctions, or pronouns. Questions about these items are integrated into the other lessons. In the first few lessons, page numbers in both *Basics* and *ExSyn* are listed with these questions to remind you to look in those chapters for the answers.

2. All numbered items are questions that need to be answered. Bullet points give you information that is useful to translation, syntactical analysis, and other aspects of the Greek text.

3. All lessons are worth at least 100 points. A few lessons are actually worth more than 100 points, with a few bonus points built in. This is because of the difficulty of the material and the potential ambiguity of the answers. The lessons that are worth more than 100 points are:

Lesson 2: Genitive	106
Lesson 5: Article, Part 1	105
Lesson 6: Article, Part 2	106
Lesson 10: Indicative Mood	102
Lesson 19: Participle, Part 2	110

4. You will notice that when a superscripted number occurs immediately after a Greek word, it is indicating which occurrence of that word in the verse is in view. Thus, for example, $ἐν^2$ indicates that the second ἐν in the verse is the one about which there is a question.

5. A frequent question will be "word related to" or "What does this modify?" These are essentially the same question. *Word related to* is asking what word—or, in some cases, phrase or clause—the word being analyzed is related to. This usually means what word (or phrase or clause) the word is modifying or is dependent on. This is an important question: syntactical connections are the backbone of exegesis.

For example, in Eph 6:1 the command is given: Τὰ τέκνα, ὑπακούετε τοῖς γονεῦσιν ὑμῶν ἐν κυρίῳ· τοῦτο γάρ ἐστιν δίκαιον ("children, obey your parents in the Lord, for this is right"). If ἐν κυρίῳ is related to γονεῦσιν, then the author is saying that as long as the parents are Christian parents, they should be obeyed. But what if they are not Christian parents—do *they* need to be obeyed? However, if ἐν κυρίῳ is related to ὑπακούετε, then the text is saying that obedience to one's parents needs to be done as an act of obedience to the Lord. Whether one's parents are Christians is not the issue, but the manner in which one responds to his or her parents is. The syntactical connection, or "word related to," is what surfaces the problem and brings the issues to a conscious level.

The easiest way to understand this question is to envision a diagram of the Greek sentence. The words that go below the base line are dependent on—and thus related to—words that are on the base line. Words that are on the base line are related to words that are to the left of them. (It should be noted that occasionally the word being analyzed will be listed with its accompanying article or adjective. In such cases, it is the noun that is under consideration. The

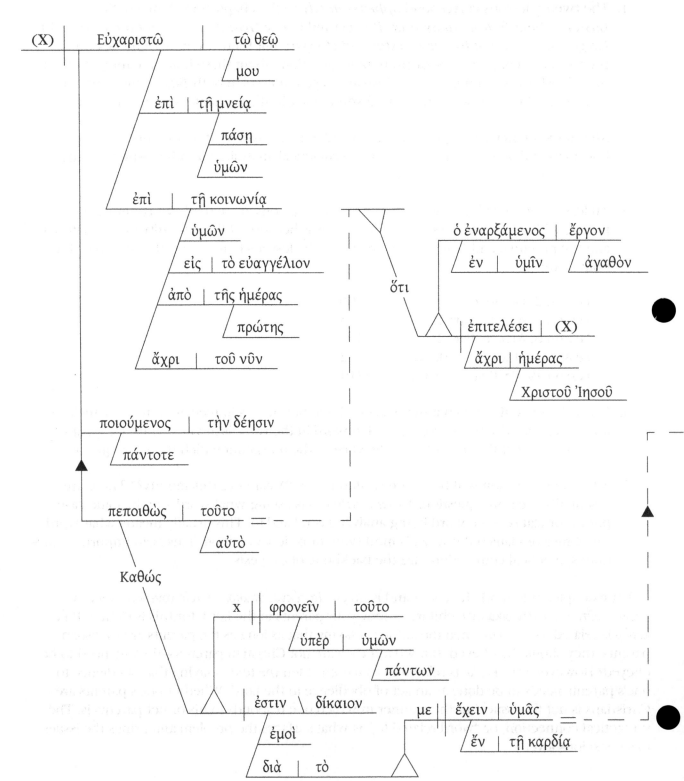

article is listed to help you readily identify which word is in view.) Thus, the direct object is related to the verb, the verb is related to the subject, etc. The lone exception to this general rule is the subject: it is related to the verb. The easiest way to think about "word related to" is to go *up* or *left* in your mental diagram. On pages 10 – 11 is a diagram of Phil 1:3–7, followed by some points about "word related to."

Philippians 1:3–7

The running Greek text of these verses is as follows:

(3) Εὐχαριστῶ τῷ θεῷ μου ἐπὶ πάσῃ τῇ μνείᾳ ὑμῶν (4) πάντοτε ἐν πάσῃ δεήσει μου ὑπὲρ πάντων ὑμῶν, μετὰ χαρᾶς τὴν δέησιν ποιούμενος, (5) ἐπὶ τῇ κοινωνίᾳ ὑμῶν εἰς τὸ εὐαγγέλιον ἀπὸ τῆς πρώτης ἡμέρας ἄχρι τοῦ νῦν, (6) πεποιθὼς αὐτὸ τοῦτο, ὅτι ὁ ἐναρξάμενος ἐν ὑμῖν ἔργον ἀγαθὸν ἐπιτελέσει ἄχρι ἡμέρας Χριστοῦ Ἰησοῦ· (7) Καθώς ἐστιν δίκαιον ἐμοὶ τοῦτο φρονεῖν ὑπὲρ πάντων ὑμῶν διὰ τὸ ἔχειν με ἐν τῇ καρδίᾳ ὑμᾶς, ἔν τε τοῖς δεσμοῖς μου καὶ ἐν τῇ ἀπολογίᾳ καὶ βεβαιώσει τοῦ εὐαγγελίου συγκοινωνούς μου τῆς χάριτος πάντας ὑμᾶς ὄντας.

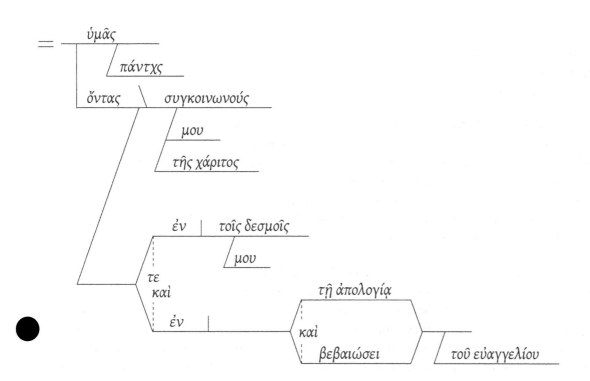

In the diagram above, vv. 3-7 are treated as one long sentence. The diagram identifies subordinate clauses and phrases visually, allowing the reader to see at a glance what is connected to what. Consider the following "word related to" questions and how easy they are to answer if one has a mental image of the diagram in front of him or her:

Verse 3

Εὐχαριστῶ—related to implied subject "I"
θεῷ—related to verb Εὐχαριστῶ
μου—related to θεῷ
μνείᾳ—related to preposition ἐπὶ
ὑμῶν—related to μνείᾳ

Verse 4

πάντοτε—related to ποιούμενος
μετά—related to ποιούμενος

Verse 5

ἐπί—related to Εὐχαριστῶ (in v. 3)
ἡμέρας—related to ἀπὸ

Verse 6

πεποιθώς—related to Εὐχαριστῶ (in v. 3)
τοῦτο—related to πεποιθὼς
αὐτό—related to τοῦτο
ὅτι—related either to τοῦτο or more generally to πεποιθὼς αὐτὸ τοῦτο

Verse 7

με—related to ἔχειν (as subject)
ὑμᾶς—related to ἔχειν (as object)
συγκοινωνούς—related to ὑμᾶς[2]

Most sentences in the Greek New Testament will not be nearly this long! But this diagram illustrates that even with complex sentences, seeing what words are related to what words is usually not difficult. A couple of minor points should be made here. First, the subject is related to the verb, even though the subject is the left-most item on the diagram's baseline. The verb is related to the subject. The predicate nominative is also related to the subject, but the direct object is related to the verb. Keeping these basic distinctions in mind will help you as you think through the connections in the Greek text.

6. You will notice that as the lessons progress, the Greek will become more difficult and the explanatory notes will become increasingly sparse. The notes are like training wheels; by the time you get to lesson 15, there are no notes. But they pick up again for later lessons because the terrain is rough and the training wheels are still needed a bit. You are encouraged to make liberal use of BDAG as you translate, especially when you come across idioms that cannot be translated in a straightforward manner into English.

It is our hope that you will understand the value of this lexicon early on, but we are nevertheless providing some helps until you get used to the format and tempo of the syntax lessons.

7. Finally, a bit of encouragement. Syntax is the backbone to exegesis. And this *Workbook* is designed to help you grasp the basic syntax of the Greek of the New Testament. It achieves this by covering virtually all the common categories of usage and by giving you samples of various texts to translate. Altogether, when you complete the *Workbook* you will have translated nearly 400 verses from the Greek New Testament taken from sixteen different books. The texts are as follows:

Matthew (51 verses)	3:1, 13; 4:1; 5:13–20; 6:26, 30; 8:15–16, 21–27; 12:32–36, 38–41; 14:27–30; 15:25–28; 16:22; 17:2–3; 21:17–21, 38; 26:20–22
Mark (28 verses)	1:14; 2:8, 16–18; 4:1–6; 9:19, 23; 13:20–21; 14:12, 32–42; 16:9
Luke (36 verses)	1:26–40; 2:36–41; 3:16; 4:4; 14:18; 17:1–6; 19:41–43; 20:3–4; 22:18
John (107 verses)	1:6–14; 2:12; 3:22; 4:1–2, 39–54; 5:16–19; 8:17–20, 34–42; 58; 9:1, 27, 30–35; 11:11–44, 49–57; 14:9; 17:7; 18:15–17, 19–22
Acts (25 verses)	3:1–10; 13:26–31; 18:18–26
Romans (16 verses)	1:7–9, 13; 2:9; 4:8; 5:1; 6:1; 9:29; 11:9–12; 14:18–19; 15:13
1 Corinthians (1 verse)	16:19
Galatians (15 verses)	2:19; 3:23–27; 6:9–17
Ephesians (26 verses)	1:13–18; 2:1–10; 3:1–10;
Philippians (39 verses)	1:1; 1:9–13, 15–30; 2:6–11; 3:1–11
Colossians (9 verses)	1:9, 13–20
1 Thessalonians (9 verses)	4:1–9
Titus (3 verses)	3:8–10
Hebrews (1 verse)	11:23
James (3 verses)	2:22; 4:7–8
1 John (9 verses)	4:8–15; 5:13
1 Peter (1 verse)	3:10
Revelation (1 verse)	9:1

Abbreviations

Basics . . . . . Daniel B. Wallace, *The Basics of New Testament Syntax.* Grand Rapids: Zondervan, 2000.

BDAG . . . . Walter Bauer, *A Greek-English Lexicon of the New Testament and Other Early Christian Literature.* 3d edition. Revised and edited by F. W. Danker. Chicago: University of Chicago Press, 2000.

BDF . . . . . F. Blass and A. Debrunner, *A Greek Grammar of the New Testament and Other Early Christian Literature.* Trans. and rev. by R. W. Funk. Chicago: University of Chicago Press, 1961.

Brown, *John* . . . . . Raymond E. Brown, *The Gospel according to John.* 2 vols. Anchor Bible 29, 29A. Garden City, NY: Doubleday, 1966 – 70.

ESV . . . . English Standard Version

ExSyn . . . . . Daniel B. Wallace, *Greek Grammar beyond the Basics: An Exegetical Syntax of the New Testament.* Grand Rapids: Zondervan, 1996.

Fanning, *Verbal Aspect* . . . . . Buist M. Fanning, *Verbal Aspect in New Testament Greek.* Oxford: Clarendon, 1990.

JTS . . . . . *Journal of Theological Studies*

LXX . . . . Septuagint

Metzger, *Textual Commentary*[2] . . . . Bruce M. Metzger, *A Textual Commentary on the Greek New Testament.* 2d edition. Stuttgart: Deutsche Bibelgesellschaft, 1994.

MS(S) . . . . manuscript(s)

NA[27] . . . . . *Novum Testament Graece,* 27th edition. Stuttgart: Deustche Bibelgesellschaft, 1993.

NET . . . . New English Translation

NET-Nestle . . . . *New English Translation*/Novum Testamentum Graece. *New Testament.* English text and notes edited by M. H. Burer, W. Hall Harris III, and D. B. Wallace. Greek text and critical apparatus of NA[27]. Dallas: NET Bible Press, 2004.

NIV . . . . New International Version

NRSV . . . . New Revised Standard Version

NT . . . . New Testament

OT . . . . Old Testament

REB . . . . Revised English Bible

Robertson, *Grammar* . . . . . A. T. Robertson, *A Grammar of the Greek New Testament in the Light of Historical Research.* 4th ed. New York: Hodder & Stoughton, 1923.

RSV . . . . Revised Standard Version

TDNT . . . . G. Kittel and G. Friedrich, eds., *Theological Dictionary of the New Testament.* Translated by G. W. Bromiley. 10 vols. Grand Rapids: Eerdmans, 1964 – 76.

TNIV . . . . Today's New International Version

TynBul . . . . . *Tyndale Bulletin*

UBS[4] . . . . United Bible Societies' *Greek New Testament,* 4th edition. Stuttgart: Deutsche Bibelgesellschaft, 1994.

Lesson 1: Nominative and Vocative

Nominative

Warm-Up Passages

Vocabulary

1. παραγίνομαι : I appear, come, arrive (Mt 3:1)	5. οἱ Φιλίπποι : Philippi (Ph 1:1)
2. ὁ βαπτιστής : Baptist (Mt 3:1)	6. ὁ ἐπίσκοπος : superintendent, guardian, bishop (Ph 1:1)
3. ἔρημος : abandoned, empty, desolate; (subst.) desert, wilderness (Mt 3:1)	7. ὁ διάκονος : servant, minister (Ph 1:1)
4. ὁ Τιμόθεος : Timothy (Ph 1:1)	

Matthew 3:1

Ἐν δὲ ταῖς ἡμέραις ἐκείναις παραγίνεται Ἰωάννης ὁ βαπτιστὴς κηρύσσων ἐν τῇ ἐρήμῳ τῆς Ἰουδαίας.

- **παραγίνεται** (This is an example of a historical present [*Basics* 226-27; *ExSyn* 526-32].)

1. **Ἰωάννης**: Case, case usage, word related to? [1+1+1]

_____

2. **ὁ βαπτιστής**: Case, case usage, word related to? [1+1+1]

_____

Philippians 1:1

Παῦλος καὶ Τιμόθεος δοῦλοι Χριστοῦ Ἰησοῦ πᾶσιν τοῖς ἁγίοις ἐν Χριστῷ Ἰησοῦ τοῖς οὖσιν ἐν Φιλίπποις σὺν ἐπισκόποις καὶ διακόνοις.

3. Παῦλος: Case, case usage? (This noun does not occur in a sentence, nor is a verb even implied. Consequently, there is no "word related to" for it. In such instances, you may be asked from time to time for the "word related to." The answer should be "no relation.") [1+1]

_____

4. Τιμόθεος: Case, case usage, word related to? [1+1+1]

_____

5. δοῦλοι: Case, case usage, word related to? [1+2+1]

_____

- πᾶσιν τοῖς ἁγίοις (This is an example of a dative of recipient, "a dative that would ordinarily be an indirect object, except that it appears in verbless constructions (such as in titles and salutations)" [*ExSyn* 148].)

Syntax Passages

John 1:6–14

Background

The Gospel of John opens with a prologue (1:1–18) in which, like Mark's Gospel, there is no genealogy and no birth narrative. But the reason for this in the Fourth Gospel is that the Son of God has always existed and, in fact, has created all things (1:1–5). His incarnation is mentioned from the divine perspective of why he came to earth (1:6–18), rather than from the human perspective of those who first beheld a newborn babe and wondered what he would become. From the outset, then, John's Gospel presents Jesus as God's Son—in fact, as God in the flesh. Our passage begins by introducing Jesus' forerunner, John the Baptist, who testifies about "the light."

Text

1:6 Ἐγένετο ἄνθρωπος, ἀπεσταλμένος παρὰ θεοῦ, ὄνομα αὐτῷ Ἰωάννης· **1:7** οὗτος ἦλθεν εἰς μαρτυρίαν ἵνα μαρτυρήσῃ περὶ τοῦ φωτός, ἵνα πάντες πιστεύσωσιν δι᾽ αὐτοῦ. **1:8** οὐκ ἦν ἐκεῖνος τὸ φῶς, ἀλλ᾽ ἵνα μαρτυρήσῃ περὶ τοῦ φωτός.

1:9 Ἦν τὸ φῶς τὸ ἀληθινόν, ὃ φωτίζει πάντα ἄνθρωπον, ἐρχόμενον εἰς τὸν κόσμον. **1:10** ἐν τῷ κόσμῳ ἦν, καὶ ὁ κόσμος δι᾽ αὐτοῦ ἐγένετο, καὶ ὁ κόσμος αὐτὸν οὐκ ἔγνω. **1:11** εἰς τὰ ἴδια ἦλθεν, καὶ οἱ ἴδιοι αὐτὸν οὐ παρέλαβον. **1:12** ὅσοι δὲ ἔλαβον αὐτόν, ἔδωκεν αὐτοῖς ἐξουσίαν τέκνα θεοῦ γενέσθαι, τοῖς πιστεύουσιν εἰς τὸ ὄνομα αὐτοῦ, **1:13** οἳ οὐκ ἐξ αἱμάτων οὐδὲ ἐκ θελήματος σαρκὸς οὐδὲ ἐκ θελήματος ἀνδρὸς ἀλλ᾽ ἐκ θεοῦ ἐγεννήθησαν.

1:14 Καὶ ὁ λόγος σὰρξ ἐγένετο καὶ ἐσκήνωσεν ἐν ἡμῖν, καὶ ἐθεασάμεθα τὴν δόξαν αὐτοῦ, δόξαν ὡς μονογενοῦς παρὰ πατρός, πλήρης χάριτος καὶ ἀληθείας.

● Vocabulary

1. ἡ μαρτυρία : testimony, witness (v. 7)	5. σκηνόω : I tabernacle, dwell (v. 14)
2. ἀληθινός : true, genuine (v. 9)	6. θεάομαι : I behold, see (v. 14)
3. φωτίζω : I shine, give light, illuminate (v. 9)	7. μονογενής : only (v. 14)
4. παραλαμβάνω : I receive, accept (v. 11)	8. πλήρης : full, filled (v. 14)

John 1:6

- ἐγένετο (In the prologue to John's Gospel [1:1-18], the author displays a tendency to use εἰμί when referring to one who exists eternally, and γίνομαι to refer to one who has a beginning. In the first five verses, εἰμί is used only in reference to God and Christ, while γίνομαι speaks of creation. When we come to v. 6, ἐγένετο ἄνθρωπος at first blush seems to mean "a man was created," especially in light of v. 3. Although this is not an appropriate rendering in this context, there does indeed seem to be a hint that the one we are looking at is a creature, a mere human.*)

6. ἄνθρωπος: Case, case usage, word related to? [1+1+1]

_____

- ἀπεσταλμένος (This use of the passive voice indicates that ἄνθρωπος receives the action expressed by the participle. The ultimate agent in this situation is indicated by παρὰ θεοῦ [*Basics* 186-87; *ExSyn* 431-33].)

7. ὄνομα: Case, case usage, word related to? [2+2+2]

_____

8. Ἰωάννης: Case, case usage, word related to? [1+1+1]

_____

---

* "This is not the *ēn*, 'was,' used of the Word in vss. 1-2, but the *egeneto* used of creation in vss. 3-4. John the Baptist is a creature" (Brown, *John*, 1.8). When we come to v. 14, how should we interpret the ἐγένετο there, which clearly refers to Christ?

John 1:7

9. οὗτος: Case, case usage, word related to? [1+1+1]

_____

- εἰς μαρτυρίαν (The preposition εἰς is probably communicating purpose here [*Basics* 166; *ExSyn* 369]. Literally it is rendered "for [a testimony].")

- μαρτυρήσῃ (This is an example of a subjunctive in a ἵνα clause expressing purpose [*Basics* 206; *ExSyn* 472].)

10. πάντες: Case, case usage, word related to? (Treat this word as a noun [*Basics* 130–31; *ExSyn* 294–95].) [1+1+1]

_____

- πιστεύσωσιν δι᾽ αὐτοῦ (Notice the care with which some prepositions are used in this passage. John's goal of testifying about Christ is that people would believe *through* him—i.e., by means of John's testimony—rather than believe in John. Jesus Christ is the object of belief in this Gospel, and the appropriate preposition after πιστεύω that speaks of belief *in* Christ is εἰς. Cf. John 1:12; 2:11; 3:16, etc. But since John is not the object of faith, διά + genitive is used here.)

John 1:8

11. ἐκεῖνος: How can you tell if this is the subject or the predicate nominative? What kind of proposition is this in—convertible or subset? [2+2]

_____

_____

12. τὸ φῶς: Case, case usage, word related to? [2+2+2]

_____

- ἀλλ᾽ ἵνα (BDF notes that an ellipsis of ἐγένετο or a similar verb can be implied by ἀλλ᾽ ἵνα [§448.7]. An appropriate gloss here would be "but [he came] in order that …").

● John 1:9

- τὸ φῶς (There are two ways to understand τὸ φῶς: (1) it can be taken as the predicate nominative related to the understood "he" that is embedded in ἦν, or (2) it can be regarded as the subject of the sentence, with ἦν as part of a periphrastic participle construction with ἐρχόμενον.)

John 1:10

13. ὁ κόσμος[2]: Case, case usage, word related to? [1+1+1]

_____

John 1:11

- τὰ ἴδια (BDAG notes that ἴδιος, when acting as a substantive, can refer to one's relatives, associates, home, possessions, or property [BDAG, s.v. ἴδιος 4]. As a neuter, which of these do you think is in view? See BDAG for help.)

● 14. οἱ ἴδιοι: Case, case usage, word related to? (Treat ἴδιοι as a noun [*Basics* 130–31; *ExSyn* 294–95].) [1+1+1]

_____

John 1:12

15. ὅσοι: In addition to being the subject of the verb ἔλαβον, what is the usage of the nominative here? Make sure and read the entire verse before answering. [2]

_____

_____

- ἐξουσίαν (BDAG notes that the use here "indicate[s] the thing that one is able to do" [BDAG, s.v. ἐξουσία 2]. Those who "receive him" have the capacity or ability to "become children of God.")

●

John 1:14

16. ὁ λόγος: Case, case usage, word related to? [1+1+1]

_____

17. σάρξ: How can you tell whether this is the predicate nominative or the subject? What kind of proposition is this—convertible or subset? [2+2]

_____

• ἐσκήνωσεν (It is possible that John is using this verb to call to mind God's dwelling among the Israelites in the OT. The implication is that, while in the OT God dwelt among the people in the tabernacle, now he is dwelling among them in the person of Jesus.)

18. ὡς: What type of conjunction is this? (Give the specific usage listed in *Basics* 293-302 or *ExSyn* 666-78.) [2]

_____

• μονογενοῦς (BDAG states that μονογενής refers to something "that is the only example of its category," and specifically in this context [v. 18] describes Jesus as "uniquely divine as God's son and transcending all others alleged to be gods" [BDAG, s.v. μονογενής 2].)

• πλήρης (Most likely the antecedent of this adjective is ὁ λόγος: "the word … [was] full of grace and truth.")

Romans 1:7-9, 13

Background

Paul opens his letter to the Romans with the longest introduction of any of his canonical works (1:1-17). In the passage below he greets the saints (1:1-7), most of whom he had never met, and expresses both thanks for them (1:8-10) and a deep desire to visit them (1:11-15).

Text

1:7 πᾶσιν τοῖς οὖσιν ἐν Ῥώμῃ ἀγαπητοῖς θεοῦ, κλητοῖς ἁγίοις, χάρις ὑμῖν καὶ εἰρήνη ἀπὸ θεοῦ πατρὸς ἡμῶν καὶ κυρίου Ἰησοῦ Χριστοῦ. **1:8** Πρῶτον μὲν εὐχαριστῶ τῷ θεῷ μου διὰ Ἰησοῦ Χριστοῦ περὶ πάντων ὑμῶν ὅτι ἡ πίστις ὑμῶν καταγγέλλεται ἐν ὅλῳ τῷ κόσμῳ. **1:9** μάρτυς γάρ μού ἐστιν ὁ θεός, ᾧ λατρεύω ἐν τῷ πνεύματί μου ἐν τῷ εὐαγγελίῳ τοῦ υἱοῦ αὐτοῦ, ὡς ἀδιαλείπτως μνείαν ὑμῶν ποιοῦμαι … **1:13** οὐ θέλω δὲ ὑμᾶς ἀγνοεῖν, ἀδελφοί, ὅτι πολλάκις προεθέμην ἐλθεῖν πρὸς ὑμᾶς, καὶ ἐκωλύθην ἄχρι τοῦ δεῦρο, ἵνα τινὰ καρπὸν σχῶ καὶ ἐν ὑμῖν καθὼς καὶ ἐν τοῖς λοιποῖς ἔθνεσιν.

● Vocabulary

1. ἡ Ῥώμη : Rome (v. 7)	8. ἡ μνεία : remembrance (v. 9)
2. κλητός : called (v. 7)	9. ἀγνοέω : I do not know, am ignorant (v. 13)
3. εὐχαριστέω : I give thanks (v. 8)	10. πολλάκις : often, many times (v. 13)
4. καταγγέλλω : I proclaim, declare (v. 8)	11. προτίθημι : I intend, plan, purpose (v. 13)
5. ὁ μάρτυς : witness (v. 9)	12. κωλύω : I hinder (v. 13)
6. λατρεύω : I serve, worship (v. 9)	13. ἄχρι : until (v. 13)
7. ἀδιαλείπτως : unceasingly (v. 9)	14. δεῦρο : now, the present (v. 13)

Romans 1:7

- πᾶσιν τοῖς οὖσιν (This is a dative of recipient, "a dative that would ordinarily be an indirect object, except that it appears in *verbless constructions* (such as in titles and salutations)" [*ExSyn* 148].)

- ἐν Ῥώμη (Some witnesses omit this phrase [G 1739[mg] 1908[mg] it[g] Origen]. Scribes might have omitted it "as the result of an accident in transcription, or, more probably, as a deliberate excision, made in order to show that the letter is of general, not local, application" [Metzger, *Textual Commentary*[2], 446].)

- θεοῦ (This is a genitive of agency, where "the genitive substantive indicates the *personal* agent by whom the action in view is accomplished" [*Basics* 61; *ExSyn* 126].)

- κλητοῖς (This is a predicate adjective in relation to ἁγίοις. κλητοῖς ἁγίοις thus is best translated "called [as] saints," or "called [to be] saints.")

19. χάρις: Case, case usage? [1+2]

_____

20. εἰρήνη: Case, case usage? (Many commentators have noted that χάρις and εἰρήνη are a combination of the common Greek and Hebrew greetings.) [1+1]

_____

Romans 1:8

- τῷ θεῷ (Dative direct object [*Basics* 78; *ExSyn* 171-72].)

- ὅτι (Conjunction, causal [*Basics* 200-201, 299; *ExSyn* 460-61, 674], or a declarative ὅτι, introducing indirect discourse and thus giving the content of Paul's thanksgiving [*Basics* 198-99; *ExSyn* 456-58].)

21. ἡ πίστις: Case, case usage, word related to? [1+1+1]

_____

Romans 1:9

22. μάρτυς: How do you know whether this is the predicate nominative or the subject? What kind of proposition is this—convertible or subset? [2+2]

_____

_____

23. ὁ θεός: Case, case usage, word related to? [1+2+2]

_____

- ἐν² (Preposition, instrumental [*Basics* 167; *ExSyn* 372-75].)

- ὡς (BDAG tells us that this conjunction can occasionally be a "marker of discourse content." Here it is giving the content of what God is witnessing [BDAG, s.v. ὡς 5].)

Romans 1:13

24. ἀδελφοί: Case, case usage, word related to? [2+2+1]

_____

- προεθέμην (Aorist of προτίθημι)

- τοῦ δεῦρο (Article substantiving an adverb and thus making it a concept: "the present time" [*Basics* 104, *ExSyn* 231-33])

- σχῶ (Aorist active subjunctive of ἔχω)

25. καί[3]: List two possible uses for this conjunction. (Look at *Basics* 293-302 or *ExSyn* 666-78.) [4]

_____

_____

Vocative

Matthew 15:25-28

Background

Matthew's Gospel records five successive withdrawals from the Jewish public by Jesus: (1) to a "deserted place," in which he still performs miracles (feeding the five thousand [14:13-21], walking on the water [14:22-33], and healing the sick at Gennesaret [14:34-36]), and cannot get away from the Pharisees (15:1-20); (2) to the region of Tyre and Sidon, where he heals a Gentile woman's daughter (15:21-28); (3) to the Sea of Galilee, where he again feeds the multitudes (15:29-38); (4) to Magadan, where he instructs his disciples about the "fluff" in the Pharisees' teaching (15:39; 16:5-12); and finally, (5) to Caesarea Philippi, where he makes it known to his disciples that he is the Christ (16:13-20). The passage below is from the second of these withdrawal narratives.

Text

15:25 ἡ δὲ ἐλθοῦσα προσεκύνει αὐτῷ λέγουσα· κύριε, βοήθει μοι.... **15:27** ἡ δὲ εἶπεν· ναὶ κύριε, καὶ γὰρ τὰ κυνάρια ἐσθίει ἀπὸ τῶν ψιχίων τῶν πιπτόντων ἀπὸ τῆς τραπέζης τῶν κυρίων αὐτῶν. **15:28** τότε ἀποκριθεὶς ὁ Ἰησοῦς εἶπεν αὐτῇ· ὦ γύναι, μεγάλη σου ἡ πίστις· γενηθήτω σοι ὡς θέλεις. καὶ ἰάθη ἡ θυγάτηρ αὐτῆς ἀπὸ τῆς ὥρας ἐκείνης.

Vocabulary

1. βοηθέω : I help (v. 25)	5. ἡ τράπεζα : table (v. 27)
2. τὸ κυνάριον : little dog, dog (v. 27)	6. Ὦ : (interjection) O! (v. 28)
3. ναί : yes, certainly, indeed (v. 27)	7. ἰάομαι : I heal (v. 28)
4. τὸ ψιχίον : very little bit, crumb (v. 27)	8. ἡ θυγάτηρ : daughter (v. 28)

Matthew 15:25

- ἡ (Article acting as a personal pronoun: "she" [*Basics* 95, *ExSyn* 211–12]. Note that only nominative articles followed by μέν or δέ may function as personal pronouns. Here the article is followed by δέ.)

- ἐλθοῦσα (This is an attendant circumstance participle. These participles are "used to communicate an action that, in some sense, is coordinate with the finite verb." It translates like a finite verb plus *and*. Here it would be rendered "she came and [bowed down]" [*Basics* 279–81, *ExSyn* 640–45 (quotation is found on 279 in *Basics* and 640 in *ExSyn*)].)

26. Κύριε: Case usage? (Vocatives are syntactically independent and consequently have "no relation" to any other word in the sentence.) [2]

Matthew 15:27

27. κύριε: Case, case usage? [1+2]

Matthew 15:28

28. ὁ Ἰησοῦς: Case, case usage, word related to? [1+1+1]

---

29. γύναι: Case, case usage? What is the exegetical significance of the usage of this case? [1+2+3]

Lesson 2: Genitive

Warm-Up Passages

Vocabulary

1. ἅπτω : I touch, take hold of (mid. with genitive) (Mt 8:15)	11. ἐπιζητέω : I search for; desire, want (Mt 12:39)
2. ὁ πυρετός : fever (Mt 8:15)	12. ὁ Ἰωνᾶς : Jonah (Mt 12:39)
3. διακονέω : I serve; minister; take care of (Mt 8:15)	13. ἡ κοιλία : belly, stomach (Mt 12:40)
4. ὄψιος : late; evening (fem. subst.) (Mt 8:16)	14. τὸ κῆτος : sea-monster (Mt 12:40)
5. προσφέρω : I bring; offer (Mt 8:16)	15. ὁ Νινευίτης : Ninevite (Mt 12:41)
6. δαιμονίζομαι : I am demon-possessed (Mt 8:16)	16. ἡ κρίσις : judgment (Mt 12:41)
7. κακῶς : bad, badly; with ἔχω, I am sick (Mt 8:16)	17. κατακρίνω : I pronounce a sentence on, judge, condemn (Mt 12:41)
8. θεραπεύω : I heal, restore (Mt 8:16)	18. μετανοέω : I repent (Mt 12:41)
9. ἡ γενεά : generation; race (Mt 12:39)	19. τὸ κήρυγμα : preaching, proclamation (Mt 12:41)
10. ἡ μοιχαλίς : adulteress; adulterous, unfaithful (adj.) (Mt 12:39)	

Matthew 8:15–16

8:15 καὶ ἥψατο τῆς χειρὸς αὐτῆς, καὶ ἀφῆκεν αὐτὴν ὁ πυρετός, καὶ ἠγέρθη καὶ διηκόνει αὐτῷ.
8:16 Ὀψίας δὲ γενομένης προσήνεγκαν αὐτῷ δαιμονιζομένους πολλούς· καὶ ἐξέβαλεν τὰ πνεύματα λόγῳ καὶ πάντας τοὺς κακῶς ἔχοντας ἐθεράπευσεν.

Matthew 8:15

1. τῆς χειρός: Case, case usage, word related to? [1+1+1]

Matthew 8:16

2. Ὀψίας: Case, case usage, word related to? [1+1+1]

Matthew 12:38–41

Background

Within the narrative concerning rising opposition to Jesus and his message (12:1–45), the religious leaders attack the source of Jesus' supernatural power (12:22–37). Immediately after Jesus' strong rebuke of the Pharisees for thinking that he is empowered by the devil (12:25–37, especially 31–32), they ironically ask for more proof concerning the source of his power (12:38). But enough miracles have been done—the sign of Jonah is all that is needed now (12:39–45).

Text

12:38 Τότε ἀπεκρίθησαν αὐτῷ τινες τῶν γραμματέων καὶ Φαρισαίων λέγοντες· διδάσκαλε, θέλομεν ἀπὸ σοῦ σημεῖον ἰδεῖν. **12:39** ὁ δὲ ἀποκριθεὶς εἶπεν αὐτοῖς· γενεὰ πονηρὰ καὶ μοιχαλὶς σημεῖον ἐπιζητεῖ, καὶ σημεῖον οὐ δοθήσεται αὐτῇ εἰ μὴ τὸ σημεῖον Ἰωνᾶ τοῦ προφήτου. **12:40** ὥσπερ γὰρ ἦν Ἰωνᾶς ἐν τῇ κοιλίᾳ τοῦ κήτους τρεῖς ἡμέρας καὶ τρεῖς νύκτας, οὕτως ἔσται ὁ υἱὸς τοῦ ἀνθρώπου ἐν τῇ καρδίᾳ τῆς γῆς τρεῖς ἡμέρας καὶ τρεῖς νύκτας. **12:41** ἄνδρες Νινευῖται ἀναστήσονται ἐν τῇ κρίσει μετὰ τῆς γενεᾶς ταύτης καὶ κατακρινοῦσιν αὐτήν, ὅτι μετενόησαν εἰς τὸ κήρυγμα Ἰωνᾶ, καὶ ἰδοὺ πλεῖον Ἰωνᾶ ὧδε.

Matthew 12:38

3. τῶν γραμματέων: Case, case usage, word related to? [1+1+1]

Matthew 12:40

4. ὥσπερ: What type of conjunction is this? (Give the specific usage listed in *Basics* 293–302 or *ExSyn* 666–78.) [2]

● Matthew 12:41

5. Ἰωνᾶ[1]: Case, case usage, word related to? (See BDAG on Ἰωνᾶς for forms.) [1+1+1]

_____

6. Ἰωνᾶ[2]: Case, case usage, word related to? [1+1+1]

_____

Syntax Passages

Luke 2:36-41

Background

The first two chapters of Luke detail the births of John the Baptist and Jesus (1:57-2:52). There are strong parallels, though with significant differences. At every point Jesus is shown to be greater than John. John's birth and infancy (1:57-80) parallel Jesus' birth and infancy (2:1-52) in the following manner: first, the mention of the birth, then the circumcision, then ● a song of praise, and finally the growth of the child. But there is contrast too: Jesus' birth is announced by angels to shepherds in a nearby field (2:8-20); at his circumcision, Anna prophesies along with Simeon's song (2:25-38); and the growth of Jesus is detailed more completely (2:41-52).

Text

2:36 Καὶ ἦν Ἅννα προφῆτις, θυγάτηρ Φανουήλ, ἐκ φυλῆς Ἀσήρ· αὕτη προβεβηκυῖα ἐν ἡμέραις πολλαῖς, ζήσασα μετὰ ἀνδρὸς ἔτη ἑπτὰ ἀπὸ τῆς παρθενίας αὐτῆς **2:37** καὶ αὐτὴ χήρα ἕως ἐτῶν ὀγδοήκοντα τεσσάρων, ἣ οὐκ ἀφίστατο τοῦ ἱεροῦ νηστείαις καὶ δεήσεσιν λατρεύουσα νύκτα καὶ ἡμέραν. **2:38** καὶ αὐτῇ τῇ ὥρᾳ ἐπιστᾶσα ἀνθωμολογεῖτο τῷ θεῷ καὶ ἐλάλει περὶ αὐτοῦ πᾶσιν τοῖς προσδεχομένοις λύτρωσιν Ἰερουσαλήμ.

2:39 Καὶ ὡς ἐτέλεσαν πάντα τὰ κατὰ τὸν νόμον κυρίου, ἐπέστρεψαν εἰς τὴν Γαλιλαίαν εἰς πόλιν ἑαυτῶν Ναζαρέθ. **2:40** Τὸ δὲ παιδίον ηὔξανεν καὶ ἐκραταιοῦτο πληρούμενον σοφίᾳ, καὶ χάρις θεοῦ ἦν ἐπ' αὐτό.

2:41 Καὶ ἐπορεύοντο οἱ γονεῖς αὐτοῦ κατ' ἔτος εἰς Ἰερουσαλὴμ τῇ ἑορτῇ τοῦ πάσχα.

Vocabulary

1. ἡ Ἅννα : Anna (v. 36)	4. ὁ Φανουήλ : Phanuel (v. 36)
2. ἡ προφῆτις : prophetess (v. 36)	5. ἡ φυλή : tribe (v. 36)
3. ἡ θυγάτηρ : daughter (lit.); female descendant (v. 36)	6. ὁ Ἀσήρ : Asher (v. 36)

7. προβαίνω : I go ahead, advance (in age, years, days) (v. 36)	18. ἀνθομολογέομαι : I praise, thank (v. 38)
8. τὸ ἔτος : year (v. 36)	19. προσδέχομαι : I take up, receive; look forward to, wait for (v. 38)
9. ἡ παρθενία : virginity (v. 36)	20. ἡ λύτρωσις : redemption, deliverance (v. 38)
10. ἡ χήρα : widow (v. 37)	21. τελέω : I bring to an end, finish (v. 39)
11. ὀγδοήκοντα : eighty (v. 37)	22. ἐπιστρέφω : I turn, return (v. 39)
12. τέσσαρες : four (v. 37)	23. ἡ Ναζαρέθ : Nazareth (v. 39)
13. ἀφίστημι : I cause to revolt; withdraw (v. 37)	24. αὐξάνω : I cause to grow, increase (v. 40)
14. ἡ νηστεία : fast, fasting (v. 37)	25. κραταιόω : I strengthen, become strong (v. 40)
15. ἡ δέησις : prayer (v. 37)	26. ὁ γονεύς : parent; parents (pl. in NT) (v. 41)
16. λατρεύω : I serve, worship (v. 37)	27. ἡ ἑορτή : festival, celebration (v. 41)
17. ἐφίστημι : I stand at or near; attack; begin; be ready (v. 38)	28. τὸ πάσχα : Passover, Passover meal (v. 41) Passover lamb

Luke 2:36

7. **Φανουήλ**: Case, case usage, word related to? (Φανουήλ is an indeclinable noun and a transliterated Hebrew proper name. Its case is determined by its function in the sentence.) [1+1+1]

• **φυλῆς** (This is a genitive object of the preposition ἐκ. Whenever a noun is the object of a preposition, you need to classify it as object of the preposition rather than think of it as a simple genitive, dative, or accusative noun. Then you can classify the preposition + case usage by consulting BDAG. (See *Basics* 162–64; *ExSyn* 360–62.)

8. **Ἀσήρ**: Case, case usage, word related to? [1+1+1]

• **προβεβηκυῖα ἐν ἡμέραις πολλαῖς** (BDAG notes that προβαίνω can be used "to make an advance in time." They also give the gloss "advance in years" [BDAG, s.v. προβαίνω 1]. BDF states in regard to ἐν ἡμέραις πολλαῖς that it carries the weight of a dative of respect. In other words it clarifies προβεβηκυῖα: "She was advancing in regard to many days." Perhaps this was a polite way of saying that she was very old [BDF, §197].)

- ἔτη (Accusative neuter plural noun from ἔτος. This is an accusative of time, which indicates extent of time. Anna had been married for an extent of seven years.)

- ἀπὸ τῆς παρθενίας (BDAG notes that it can refer to "the time of virginity [w. focus on time of entry into married status]" [BDAG, s.v. παρθενία]. The idea here would therefore be that Anna had been married seven years. The "time of her virginity," refers to her single status prior to being married.)

Luke 2:37

- χήρα (predicate nominative related to an implied εἰμί)

- ἕως ἐτῶν ὀγδοήκοντα τεσσάρων (BDAG gives the translation "until she was now 84 years old" [BDAG, s.v. ἕως].)

9. τοῦ ἱεροῦ: Case, case usage, word related to? [1+1+1]

- νηστείαις καὶ δεήσεσιν (datives of manner related to λατρεύουσα [cf. *Basics* 74-75; *ExSyn* 161-62])

- λατρεύουσα (adverbial participle of cause or contemporaneous time [cf. *Basics*: 272-73, 275-76; *ExSyn* 623-27, 631-32)

10. νύκτα καὶ ἡμέραν: (These are accusatives of measure/time related to λατρεύουσα [cf. *Basics* 90; *ExSyn* 201-203]. Since they are accusatives of time, they describe the extent or duration of time. Anna was worshiping every night and every day.) What if these nouns had been in the genitive case instead of the accusative (νυκτὸς καὶ ἡμέρας)? How would the meaning be different? [2]

Luke 2:38

- αὐτῇ τῇ ὥρᾳ (The noun ὥρα is a dative of measure/time [cf. *Basics* 72-73; *ExSyn* 155-57]. It signals a point in time. The αὐτῇ is in the predicate position and should be translated as an intensifier [cf. *Basics* 155; *ExSyn* 348-50]. This is woodenly rendered "at the hour itself"; more idiomatically, "at that very moment."

- ἐπιστᾶσα (This is an attendant circumstance participle. These participles are "used to communicate an action that, in some sense, is coordinate with the finite verb." It can be translated like a finite verb plus *and*. Here it would be rendered, "she came and [began to give thanks]" [*ExSyn* 640; cf. *Basics* 279-81; *ExSyn* 640-45].)

11. Ἰερουσαλήμ: Case, case usage, word related to? [1+1+1]

_____

Luke 2:39

12. ὡς: What type of conjunction is this? (Give the specific usage listed in *Basics* 293–302 or *ExSyn* 666–78.) [2]

_____

- τά: (The article is substantizing the prepositional phrase κατὰ τὸν νόμον κυρίου [cf. *Basics* 105; *ExSyn* 236]. It can be translated "the things [according to the law of the Lord].")

13. κυρίου: Case, case usage, word related to? [1+1+1]

_____

14. ἑαυτῶν: Case, case usage, word related to? [1+1+1]

_____

15. Ναζαρέθ: Case, case usage, word related to? [1+1+1]

_____

Luke 2:40

16. θεοῦ: Case, case usage? [1+1]

_____

Luke 2:41

17. αὐτοῦ: Case, case usage? [1+1]

_____

18. **τοῦ πάσχα**: Case, case usage, word related to? [1+1+1]

Ephesians 1:13-18

Background

This letter begins with praise for God as a theological preface to the body of the letter (1:3-14): God is blessed and is to be praised because (1) the Father elected them in eternity past (1:3-6), the Son redeemed them in the historical past (1:7-12), and the Spirit sealed them in their personal and individual pasts (1:13-14). Thus the letter begins with a reminder of the great things God has done for them individually. With this as a backdrop, a prayer is offered up that the readers will understand what God has done for them corporately (1:15-23).

Text

1:13 Ἐν ᾧ καὶ ὑμεῖς ἀκούσαντες τὸν λόγον τῆς ἀληθείας, τὸ εὐαγγέλιον τῆς σωτηρίας ὑμῶν, ἐν ᾧ καὶ πιστεύσαντες ἐσφραγίσθητε τῷ πνεύματι τῆς ἐπαγγελίας τῷ ἁγίῳ, **1:14** ὅς ἐστιν ἀρραβὼν τῆς κληρονομίας ἡμῶν, εἰς ἀπολύτρωσιν τῆς περιποιήσεως, εἰς ἔπαινον τῆς δόξης αὐτοῦ.

1:15 Διὰ τοῦτο κἀγώ ἀκούσας τὴν καθ' ὑμᾶς πίστιν ἐν τῷ κυρίῳ Ἰησοῦ καὶ τὴν ἀγάπην τὴν εἰς πάντας τοὺς ἁγίους **1:16** οὐ παύομαι εὐχαριστῶν ὑπὲρ ὑμῶν μνείαν ποιούμενος ἐπὶ τῶν προσευχῶν μου, **1:17** ἵνα ὁ θεὸς τοῦ κυρίου ἡμῶν Ἰησοῦ Χριστοῦ, ὁ πατὴρ τῆς δόξης, δώῃ ὑμῖν πνεῦμα σοφίας καὶ ἀποκαλύψεως ἐν ἐπιγνώσει αὐτοῦ, **1:18** πεφωτισμένους τοὺς ὀφθαλμοὺς τῆς καρδίας ὑμῶν εἰς τὸ εἰδέναι ὑμᾶς τίς ἐστιν ἡ ἐλπὶς τῆς κλήσεως αὐτοῦ, τίς ὁ πλοῦτος τῆς δόξης τῆς κληρονομίας αὐτοῦ ἐν τοῖς ἁγίοις.

Vocabulary

1. ἡ σωτηρία : deliverance; salvation (v. 13)	9. εὐχαριστέω : I give thanks, thank (v. 16)
2. σφραγίζω : I seal; seal up; certify (v. 13)	10. ἡ μνεία : memory, remembrance (v. 16)
3. ὁ ἀρραβών : first installment, deposit (v. 14)	11. ἡ προσευχή : prayer (v. 16)
4. ἡ κληρονομία : inheritance, possession (v. 14)	12. ἡ ἀποκάλυψις : revelation, disclosure (v. 17)
5. ἡ ἀπολύτρωσις : release; redemption; deliverance (v. 14)	13. ἡ ἐπίγνωσις : knowledge, recognition (v. 17)
6. ἡ περιποίησις : property; possession (v. 14)	14. φωτίζω : I illuminate; enlighten (v. 18)
7. ὁ ἔπαινος : praise, approval, fame (v. 14)	15. ἡ κλῆσις : call, calling (v. 18)
8. παύω : I cease; cause to stop, hinder (v. 16)	16. ὁ, τὸ πλοῦτος : riches; wealth; abundance (v. 18)

Ephesians 1:13

- ἐν ᾧ (Here the preposition with the dative relative pronoun refers back to Christ in v. 12. This should be translated "in whom.")

- καί (This is an adjunctive example of a connective conjunction [cf. *Basics* 296; *ExSyn* 671]. It is being used emphatically and should be translated "also.")

19. τῆς ἀληθείας: Case, case usage, word related to? [1+1+1]

_____

20. τῆς σωτηρίας: Case, case usage, word related to? [1+1+1]

_____

21. ὑμῶν: Case, case usage? [1+1]

_____

22. τῆς ἐπαγγελίας: Case, case usage, word related to? [1+1+1]

_____

Ephesians 1:14

- ὅ (relative pronoun, referring back to πνεύματι in v. 13; the gender is neuter because πνεύματι is neuter. Some MSS have masculine ὅς here, because it is attracted to the gender of the PN in v. 14, ἀρραβών)

23. τῆς κληρονομίας: Case, case usage, word related to? [1+1+1]

_____

24. ἡμῶν: Case, case usage, word related to? [1+1+1]

_____

- τῆς περιποιήσεως (Genitive, objective, ἀπολύτρωσιν)

- αὐτοῦ (This is a genitive of possession related to δόξης.)

● Ephesians 1:16

- εὐχαριστῶν (This is a complementary participle related to παύομαι. The complementary participle "completes the thought of another verb" [*ExSyn* 646].)

25. ὑμῶν² (The majority of MSS list a second ὑμῶν after μνείαν. It is probably not authentic. More than likely the second pronoun was a scribal addition to help clarify the meaning of the text. What would the syntactical function of the second ὑμῶν be and how would it clarify the text?) [2+2]

_____

_____

26. τῶν προσευχῶν: Case, case usage, word related to? [1+1+1]

_____

27. μου: Case, case usage, word related to? [1+1+1]

●
_____

Ephesians 1:17

- ἵνα (This is a conjunction communicating purpose or result [cf. *Basics* 206-7; *ExSyn* 473-74].)

28. τοῦ κυρίου: Case, case usage, word related to? [1+1+1]

_____

29. ἡμῶν: Case, case usage? [1+1]

_____

30. Ἰησοῦ Χριστοῦ: Case, case usage, word related to? [1+1+1]

_____

31. τῆς δόξης: Case, case usage, word related to? [1+1+1]

●
_____

- δώη (This verb is in the subjunctive mood and is communicating purpose or result with the ἵνα clause [cf. *Basics* 206-7; *ExSyn* 473-74].)

32. σοφίας: Case, case usage, word related to? [1+1+1]

_____

33. ἀποκαλύψεως: Case, case usage, word related to? [1+2+1]

_____

- αὐτοῦ (Genitive, objective, ἐπιγνώσει)

Ephesians 1:18

- τῆς καρδίας (Genitive, possessive or possibly partitive [in a figurative sense], ὀφθαλμούς)

- εἰς τὸ εἰδέναι (This is an infinitive of purpose or result related to πεφωτισμένους [cf. *Basics* 256-58; *ExSyn* 590-94].)

- τίς (This interrogative pronoun is functioning as the predicate nominative of ἐστιν.)

34. τῆς κλήσεως: Case, case usage, word related to? [1+1+1]

_____

35. αὐτοῦ: Case, case usage, word related to? [1+1+1]

_____

- τίς ὁ πλοῦτος (This is the same kind of construction that we saw in τίς ἐστιν ἡ ἐλπίς.)

36. τῆς δόξης: Case, case usage, word related to? [1+1+1]

_____

37. τῆς κληρονομίας: Case, case usage, word related to? [1+1+1]

_____

Lesson 3: Dative

Warm-Up Passages

Vocabulary

1. ἄζυμος : festival of unleavened bread (subst.) (Mk 14:12)	5. ἑτοιμάζω : I prepare (Mk 14:12)
2. τὸ πάσχα : Passover, Passover meal, Passover lamb (Mk 14:12)	6. δουλεύω : I am a slave, serve, obey (Ro 14:18)
3. θύω : I sacrifice, slaughter, kill, celebrate (Mk 14:12)	7. εὐάρεστος : pleasing, acceptable (Ro 14:18)
4. ποῦ : where? (Mk 14:12)	8. δόκιμος : approved, genuine; respected, esteemed (Ro 14:18)

Mark 14:12

Καὶ τῇ πρώτῃ ἡμέρᾳ τῶν ἀζύμων, ὅτε τὸ πάσχα ἔθυον, λέγουσιν αὐτῷ οἱ μαθηταὶ αὐτοῦ· ποῦ θέλεις ἀπελθόντες ἑτοιμάσωμεν ἵνα φάγῃς τὸ πάσχα;

1. ἡμέρᾳ: Case, case usage, word related to? [1+1+1]

ἀπελθόντες (This is a complementary participle related to θέλεις. The complementary participle "*completes* the thought of another verb" [*ExSyn* 646]. A complementary infinitive would have been expected after a verb of wishing or desire [θέλω, βούλομαι, ὀφείλω]. A participle with these verbs is rare [cf. Acts 25:9, Jude 5].)

Luke 3:16

Ἐγὼ μὲν ὕδατι βαπτίζω ὑμᾶς.

2. ὕδατι: Case, case usage, word related to? [1+1+1]

Romans 14:18

ὁ γὰρ ἐν τούτῳ δουλεύων τῷ Χριστῷ εὐάρεστος τῷ θεῷ καὶ δόκιμος τοῖς ἀνθρώποις.

3. τούτῳ: Case, case usage, word related to? [1+1+1]

_____

4. τῷ Χριστῷ: Case, case usage, word related to? [1+1+1]

_____

5. τῷ θεῷ: Case, case usage, word related to? [1+1+1]

_____

6. τοῖς ἀνθρώποις: Case, case usage, word related to? (It might be tempting to classify this as a dative of agency. Remember that the dative of agency is "an extremely rare category in the NT, as well as in ancient Greek in general" [*ExSyn* 163].) What are some reasons why this should not be taken as a dative of agency (see discussion in *Basics* 75-77 or *ExSyn* 163-66)? [1+1+1+2]

_____

_____

Syntax Passages

John 18:15-17, 19-22

Background

John 18 brings us to the passion of Christ, speaking of his arrest after being betrayed by Judas (18:1-11), trial before Annas and Caiaphas (18:12-27), and trial before Pilate (18:28-40).

Text

18:15 Ἠκολούθει δὲ τῷ Ἰησοῦ Σίμων Πέτρος καὶ ἄλλος μαθητής. ὁ δὲ μαθητὴς ἐκεῖνος ἦν γνωστὸς τῷ ἀρχιερεῖ καὶ συνεισῆλθεν τῷ Ἰησοῦ εἰς τὴν αὐλὴν τοῦ ἀρχιερέως, **18:16** ὁ δὲ Πέτρος εἱστήκει πρὸς τῇ θύρᾳ ἔξω. ἐξῆλθεν οὖν ὁ μαθητὴς ὁ ἄλλος ὁ γνωστὸς τοῦ ἀρχιερέως καὶ εἶπεν τῇ θυρωρῷ καὶ εἰσήγαγεν τὸν Πέτρον. **18:17** λέγει οὖν τῷ Πέτρῳ ἡ παιδίσκη ἡ θυρωρός· μὴ καὶ σὺ ἐκ τῶν μαθητῶν εἶ τοῦ ἀνθρώπου τούτου; λέγει ἐκεῖνος· οὐκ εἰμί.…

18:19 Ὁ οὖν ἀρχιερεὺς ἠρώτησεν τὸν Ἰησοῦν περὶ τῶν μαθητῶν αὐτοῦ καὶ περὶ τῆς διδαχῆς αὐτοῦ. **18:20** ἀπεκρίθη αὐτῷ Ἰησοῦς· ἐγὼ παρρησίᾳ λελάληκα τῷ κόσμῳ, ἐγὼ πάντοτε ἐδίδαξα ἐν συναγωγῇ καὶ ἐν τῷ ἱερῷ, ὅπου πάντες οἱ Ἰουδαῖοι συνέρχονται, καὶ ἐν κρυπτῷ ἐλάλησα οὐδέν. **18:21** τί με ἐρωτᾷς; ἐρώτησον τοὺς ἀκηκοότας τί ἐλάλησα αὐτοῖς· ἴδε οὗτοι οἴδασιν ἃ εἶπον ἐγώ. **18:22** ταῦτα δὲ αὐτοῦ εἰπόντος εἷς παρεστηκὼς τῶν ὑπηρετῶν ἔδωκεν ῥάπισμα τῷ Ἰησοῦ εἰπών· οὕτως ἀποκρίνῃ τῷ ἀρχιερεῖ;

Vocabulary

1. γνωστός : known; acquaintance, friend (subst.) (v. 15)	9. ἡ παρρησία : confidence, boldness, outspokenness, openness (v. 20)
2. συνεισέρχομαι : I enter or go in(to) with (v. 15)	10. πάντοτε : always, at all times (v. 20)
3. ἡ αὐλή : courtyard, court (v. 15)	11. συνέρχομαι : I assemble, gather, come together with (v. 20)
4. ἡ θύρα : door (v. 16)	12. κρυπτός : hidden, secret (v. 20)
5. ὁ θυρωρός : doorkeeper, gatekeeper (v. 16)	13. ἴδε : look, see, behold (v. 21)
6. εἰσάγω : I bring in or into, lead in or into (v. 16)	14. παρίστημι : I stand by, stand near; place beside (v. 22)
7. ἡ παιδίσκη : female slave, slave (v. 17)	15. ὁ ὑπηρέτης : helper, assistant, minister (v. 22)
8. ἡ διδαχή : teaching, instruction (v. 19)	16. τὸ ῥάπισμα : slap in the face; blow (v. 22)

John 18:15

7. τῷ Ἰησοῦ[1]: Case, case usage, word related to? [1+1+1]

_____

8. τῷ ἀρχιερεῖ: Case, case usage, word related to? [1+2+2]

_____

9. τῷ Ἰησοῦ[2]: Case, case usage, word related to? [1+2+1]

_____

John 18:16

10. τῇ θύρᾳ: Case, case usage, word related to? [1+1+1]

_____

11. τῇ θυρωρῷ: Case, case usage, word related to? [1+1+1]

_____

John 18:17

12. τῷ Πέτρῳ: Case, case usage, word related to? (The direct object for this word is the servant girl's statement.) [1+1+1]

_____

- Μή (A question prefaced by μή expects a negative answer.)

John 18:19

13. οὖν: What type of conjunction is this? (Give the specific usage listed in *Basics* 293–302 or *ExSyn* 666–78.) [2]

_____

John 18:20

14. παρρησίᾳ: Case, case usage, word related to? [1+2+1]

_____

15. τῷ κόσμῳ: Case, case usage, word related to? [1+1+1]

_____

John 18:22

- παρεστηκώς (This is an attributive participle modifying εἷς [cf. *Basics* 270; *ExSyn* 617–19].)

- τῶν ὑπηρετῶν (This partitive gentive is modifying εἷς [cf. *Basics* 48; *ExSyn* 84–86].)

16. τῷ Ἰησοῦ: Case, case usage, word related to? (Other than indirect object, what is the best way to categorize this noun?) [1+2+1]

_____

17. τῷ ἀρχιερεῖ: Case, case usage, word related to? [1+1+1]

Galatians 6:9-17

Background

True liberty, Paul says, is liberty to love and to serve others (6:1-10). The spiritual should serve by gently rebuking the weak and modeling responsibility for the corporate body of Christ (6:1-5). The congregation should exercise its liberty by loving all people, but especially other believers (6:10). Paul closes his epistle (6:11-18) by unmasking the true motives of the Judaizers (6:12-13) as compared with his own motives (6:14-17), followed by his customary benediction (6:18).

Text

6:9 τὸ δὲ καλὸν ποιοῦντες μὴ ἐγκακῶμεν, καιρῷ γὰρ ἰδίῳ θερίσομεν μὴ ἐκλυόμενοι. **6:10** Ἄρα οὖν ὡς καιρὸν ἔχομεν, ἐργαζώμεθα τὸ ἀγαθὸν πρὸς πάντας, μάλιστα δὲ πρὸς τοὺς οἰκείους τῆς πίστεως.

6:11 Ἴδετε πηλίκοις ὑμῖν γράμμασιν ἔγραψα τῇ ἐμῇ χειρί. **6:12** Ὅσοι θέλουσιν εὐπροσωπῆσαι ἐν σαρκί, οὗτοι ἀναγκάζουσιν ὑμᾶς περιτέμνεσθαι, μόνον ἵνα τῷ σταυρῷ τοῦ Χριστοῦ μὴ διώκωνται. **6:13** οὐδὲ γὰρ οἱ περιτεμνόμενοι αὐτοὶ νόμον φυλάσσουσιν ἀλλὰ θέλουσιν ὑμᾶς περιτέμνεσθαι, ἵνα ἐν τῇ ὑμετέρᾳ σαρκὶ καυχήσωνται. **6:14** Ἐμοὶ δὲ μὴ γένοιτο καυχᾶσθαι εἰ μὴ ἐν τῷ σταυρῷ τοῦ κυρίου ἡμῶν Ἰησοῦ Χριστοῦ, δι᾽ οὗ ἐμοὶ κόσμος ἐσταύρωται κἀγὼ κόσμῳ. **6:15** οὔτε γὰρ περιτομή τί ἐστιν οὔτε ἀκροβυστία ἀλλὰ καινὴ κτίσις. **6:16** καὶ ὅσοι τῷ κανόνι τούτῳ στοιχήσουσιν, εἰρήνη ἐπ᾽ αὐτοὺς καὶ ἔλεος καὶ ἐπὶ τὸν Ἰσραὴλ τοῦ θεοῦ.

6:17 Τοῦ λοιποῦ κόπους μοι μηδεὶς παρεχέτω· ἐγὼ γὰρ τὰ στίγματα τοῦ Ἰησοῦ ἐν τῷ σώματί μου βαστάζω.

Vocabulary

1. ἐγκακέω : I lose enthusiasm or heart, be discouraged (v. 9)	16. φυλάσσω : I watch, guard; obey (v. 13)
2. θερίζω : I harvest; reap (v. 9)	17. ὑμέτερος : your (pl.) (v. 13)
3. ἐκλύω : I become weary, give out, lose heart (pass. in NT) (v. 9)	18. καυχάομαι : I boast, brag (v. 13)
4. ἄρα : therefore, so then (v. 10)	19. ἡ περιτομή : circumcision, those who are circumcised, Jews (v. 15)
5. ἐργάζομαι : I toil, do, labor for (v. 10)	20. ἡ ἀκροβυστία : uncircumcision, Gentile (fig.) (v. 15)

6. μάλιστα : most of all, above all (v. 10)	21. καινός : new (v. 15)
7. οἰκεῖος : member of a household (subst. in NT) (v. 10)	22. ἡ κτίσις : creation, creature, world (v. 15)
8. πηλίκος : how large; how great (v. 11)	23. ὁ κανών : rule, standard (v. 16)
9. τὸ γράμμα : letter (of the alphabet); document, letter (v. 11)	24. στοιχέω : I agree with, hold to, follow (v. 16)
10. εὐπροσωπέω : I make a good showing (v. 12)	25. τὸ ἔλεος : mercy, compassion, pity (v. 16)
11. ἀναγκάζω : I compel, force (v. 12)	26. ὁ κόπος : trouble, difficulty; work, labor (v. 17)
12. περιτέμνω : I circumcise (lit. and fig.) (v. 12)	27. παρέχω : I cause trouble (with κόπος) (v. 17)
13. ὁ σταυρός : cross (fig. and lit.) (v. 12)	28. τὸ στίγμα : mark, brand (v. 17)
14. σταυρόω : I crucify (lit. and fig.) (v. 12)	29. βαστάζω : bear, carry (v. 17)
15. διώκω : I persecute; pursue (v. 12)	

Galatians 6:9

- **ποιοῦντες** (This is a complementary participle related to ἐγκακῶμεν [cf. *ExSyn* 646].)

18. **καιρῷ**: Case, case usage, word related to? [1+1+1]

Galatians 6:10

- **ἄρα οὖν** (BDAG states that ἄρα can "express result" [BDAG, s.v. ἄρα 2.b]. BDF adds to this that ἄρα is "strengthened by οὖν" [BDF §451.2b]. Thus this is an emphatic way of expressing result.)

- **ὡς** (This is a temporal conjunction that should be rendered "when" [cf. *Basics* 301; *ExSyn* 677].)

- **καιρόν** (the direct object of ἔχομεν [cf. *Basics* 83; *ExSyn* 179–81])

Galatians 6:11

- **πηλίκοις** (This word modifies γράμμασιν and should be rendered "how great" or "how large.")

19. ὑμῖν: Case, case usage, word related to? [1+1+1]

_____

20. γράμμασιν: Case, case usage, word related to? [1+2+1]

_____

21. χειρί: Case, case usage, word related to? [1+2+1]

_____

Galatians 6:12

22. ἐν σαρκί: Case, force of phrase? (Answer this question as if the preposition were not present and the text simply read σαρκί.) [1+2]

_____

• ἵνα ... μὴ διώκωνται (This ἵνα clause is communicating purpose, "so that they might not be persecuted" [cf. *Basics* 206-7; *ExSyn* 472].)

23. τῷ σταυρῷ: Case, case usage, word related to? [1+2+1]

_____

Galatians 6:14

24. ἐμοί[1]: Case, case usage, word related to? [1+2+1]

_____

• μὴ γένοιτο (BDF states that μὴ γένοιτο [an optative verb form] is used "to express strong rejection" [BDF §384]. It can be rendered "may it never be.")

25. ἐμοί[2]: Case, case usage, word related to? [1+2+1]

_____

26. **κόσμῳ**: Case, case usage, word related to? (Notice that κόσμῳ is connected to ἐμοί[2] by a form of καί. When words are in this sort of parallel connected by καί they typically have the same syntactical function in prose. The situation is different in poetry, where an author is given more liberty to diverge from such expectations for the sake of rhetorical effect.) [1+1+1]

Galatians 6:15

- **οὔτε γάρ** (The majority of MSS have the reading ἐν γὰρ Χριστῷ Ἰησοῦ οὔτε instead of the shorter reading, οὔτε γάρ. The longer reading should not be accepted for two reasons. First, there is still strong support for the simple οὔτε γάρ [P[46] B Ψ 075 33 1175 1739* it[r] (syr[p, pal]) cop[samss] arm[mss] geo[1]]. Second, the principle of *lectio brevior lectio potior* ["the shorter reading is the more probable reading"] is operative here. The longer reading was almost surely an attempt by scribes to clarify the meaning of the text.)

27. **οὔτε[1]**: What type of conjunction is this? [3] (Give the specific usage listed in *Basics* 293–302 or *ExSyn* 666–78.)

- **τί** (This is an indefinite pronoun and should be rendered "anything" [cf. *Basics* 154; *ExSyn* 347]. The reason for the acute accent is that the following word, ἐστιν, is an enclitic and is thus considered a part of the preceding word as far as accenting is concerned.)

Galatians 6:16

28. **τῷ κανόνι**: Case, case usage, word related to? [1+2+1]

Galatians 6:17

- **Τοῦ λοιποῦ** (BDAG notes that this word can occasionally have an adverbial force. They give a few glosses, "from now on, in the future, henceforth" [BDAG, s.v. λοιπός 3.a].

29. **μοι**: Case, case usage, word related to? [1+2+1]

Lesson 4: Accusative

Warm-Up Passages

Vocabulary

1. ἡ Καφαρναούμ : Capernaum (Jn 2:12)	2. τὸ βάπτισμα : plunging, dipping, washing, baptism (Lk 20:4)

John 2:12

Μετὰ τοῦτο κατέβη εἰς Καφαρναοὺμ αὐτὸς καὶ ἡ μήτηρ αὐτοῦ καὶ οἱ ἀδελφοὶ αὐτοῦ καὶ οἱ μαθηταὶ αὐτοῦ καὶ ἐκεῖ ἔμειναν οὐ πολλὰς ἡμέρας.

1. ἡμέρας: Case, case usage, word related to? [1+1+1]

_____

Luke 20:3–4

20:3 ἀποκριθεὶς δὲ εἶπεν πρὸς αὐτούς· ἐρωτήσω ὑμᾶς κἀγὼ λόγον, καὶ εἴπατέ μοι· **20:4** τὸ βάπτισμα Ἰωάννου ἐξ οὐρανοῦ ἦν ἢ ἐξ ἀνθρώπων;

2. ὑμᾶς: Case, case usage, word related to? [1+1+1]

_____

3. λόγον: Case, case usage, word related to? [1+1+1]

_____

Syntax Passages

Philippians 3:1-11

Background

Paul here articulates the basis that the Judaizers were resting on: the works of the flesh (3:1-2). He then points out that he would have a greater claim to boast in the flesh than they since he had the proper Jewish credentials (3:3-6). Yet Paul does not boast; in fact, he very graphically explains that the only thing the flesh can produce is worthless (3:7-11; especially

43

v. 8). The basis of his righteousness, therefore, is the faithfulness of Christ/faith in Christ (3:9), and the goal is Christ's resurrection power (3:10-11).

Text

3:1 Τὸ λοιπόν, ἀδελφοί μου, χαίρετε ἐν κυρίῳ. τὰ αὐτὰ γράφειν ὑμῖν ἐμοὶ μὲν οὐκ ὀκνηρόν, ὑμῖν δὲ ἀσφαλές.

3:2 Βλέπετε τοὺς κύνας, βλέπετε τοὺς κακοὺς ἐργάτας, βλέπετε τὴν κατατομήν. **3:3** ἡμεῖς γάρ ἐσμεν ἡ περιτομή, οἱ πνεύματι θεοῦ λατρεύοντες καὶ καυχώμενοι ἐν Χριστῷ Ἰησοῦ καὶ οὐκ ἐν σαρκὶ πεποιθότες, **3:4** καίπερ ἐγὼ ἔχων πεποίθησιν καὶ ἐν σαρκί. Εἴ τις δοκεῖ ἄλλος πεποιθέναι ἐν σαρκί, ἐγὼ μᾶλλον· **3:5** περιτομῇ ὀκταήμερος, ἐκ γένους Ἰσραήλ, φυλῆς Βενιαμίν, Ἑβραῖος ἐξ Ἑβραίων, κατὰ νόμον Φαρισαῖος, **3:6** κατὰ ζῆλος διώκων τὴν ἐκκλησίαν, κατὰ δικαιοσύνην τὴν ἐν νόμῳ γενόμενος ἄμεμπτος. **3:7** Ἀλλὰ ἅτινα ἦν μοι κέρδη, ταῦτα ἥγημαι διὰ τὸν Χριστὸν ζημίαν. **3:8** ἀλλὰ μενοῦνγε καὶ ἡγοῦμαι πάντα ζημίαν εἶναι διὰ τὸ ὑπερέχον τῆς γνώσεως Χριστοῦ Ἰησοῦ τοῦ κυρίου μου, δι' ὃν τὰ πάντα ἐζημιώθην, καὶ ἡγοῦμαι σκύβαλα, ἵνα Χριστὸν κερδήσω **3:9** καὶ εὑρεθῶ ἐν αὐτῷ, μὴ ἔχων ἐμὴν δικαιοσύνην τὴν ἐκ νόμου ἀλλὰ τὴν διὰ πίστεως Χριστοῦ, τὴν ἐκ θεοῦ δικαιοσύνην ἐπὶ τῇ πίστει, **3:10** τοῦ γνῶναι αὐτὸν καὶ τὴν δύναμιν τῆς ἀναστάσεως αὐτοῦ καὶ τὴν κοινωνίαν τῶν παθημάτων αὐτοῦ, συμμορφιζόμενος τῷ θανάτῳ αὐτοῦ, **3:11** εἴ πως καταντήσω εἰς τὴν ἐξανάστασιν τὴν ἐκ νεκρῶν.

Vocabulary

1. ὀκνηρός : troublesome; idle, lazy (v. 1)	18. ἄμεμπτος : blameless, faultless (v. 6)
2. ἀσφαλής : firm, safe (v. 1)	19. τὸ κέρδος : gain, profit (v. 7)
3. ὁ κύων : dog; unqualified person (fig.) (v. 2)	20. ἡγέομαι : I think, consider, regard (v. 7)
4. ὁ ἐργάτης : workman, laborer (v. 2)	21. ἡ ζημία : damage, loss, forfeit (v. 7)
5. ἡ κατατομή : mutilation, cutting in pieces (v. 2)	22. μενοῦνγε : rather, on the contrary (v. 8)
6. ἡ περιτομή : circumcision (v. 3)	23. ὑπερέχω : I have power over; surpass; surpassing greatness (subst.) (v. 8)
7. λατρεύω : I serve, worship (v. 3)	24. ἡ γνῶσις : knowledge, comprehension (v. 8)
8. καυχάομαι : I boast, brag (v. 3)	25. ζημιόω : I suffer damage, loss, forfeit (pass. in NT) (v. 8)
9. καίπερ : although (v. 4)	26. τὸ σκύβαλον : refuse, garbage, crud (v. 8)
10. ἡ πεποίθησις : trust, confidence (v. 4)	27. κερδαίνω : I gain, profit (v. 8)
11. ὀκταήμερος : on the eighth day (v. 5)	28. ἡ ἀνάστασις : resurrection (v. 10)

12. τὸ γένος : descendant; family; nation (v. 5)	29. ἡ κοινωνία : fellowship, communion, unity (v. 10)
13. ἡ φυλή : tribe (v. 5)	30. τὸ πάθημα : suffering, misfortune (v. 10)
14. ὁ Βενιαμίν : Benjamin (v. 5)	31. συμμορφίζω : I take on the same form as, am conformed to (v. 10)
15. ὁ Ἑβραῖος : Hebrew (v. 5)	32. πώς : somehow, in some way, perhaps (v. 11)
16. ὁ ζῆλος : zeal, ardor; jealousy, envy (v. 6)	33. καταντάω : I come (to), arrive (to), reach (v. 11)
17. διώκω : I persecute; pursue (v. 6)	34. ἡ ἐξανάστασις : resurrection (v. 11)

Philippians 3:1

4. τὸ λοιπόν: Case, case usage, word related to? [1+2+1]

_____

5. τὰ αὐτά: Case, case usage, word related to? [1+2+2]

_____

- γράφειν (This infinitive is the subject of an implied εἰμί with οὐκ ὀκνηρόν as the predicate nominative. It can be rendered, "To write [the same things is no trouble for me]" [cf. *Basics* 260-61; *ExSyn* 600-601].)

Philippians 3:2

- βλέπετε: (Here βλέπω is in the imperative and is being used to command the Philippians to watch out for something that is potentially hazardous. An appropriate gloss would be "watch out for" or "beware of" [BDAG, βλέπω s.v. 5].)

6. τοὺς κύνας: Case, case usage, word related to? [1+1+1]

_____

Philippians 3:3

- θεοῦ (The verb λατρεύω normally takes a dative direct object. This could potentially make πνεύματι the object of λατρεύοντες, emphasizing the worship of the Spirit. Although πνεύματι most likely has an instrumental force ["by the Spirit"], several ancient witnesses clarified the issue by substituting θεῷ for θεοῦ [so ℵ² D* Ψ 075 365 1175 lat sy Chr]. The most reliable papyrus for Paul [P⁴⁶] virtually stands alone in omitting either form of "God." Other ancient MSS have the genitive θεοῦ [ℵ* A B C D² G 33 81 614 1739 itᵍ syrʰᵐᵍ copˢᵃ, ᵇᵒ al.]. Given the strong external support for this reading, it is best to see its omission as accidental and the substitution of θεῷ as theologically motivated.)

Philippians 3:4

- ἔχων (Moule notes that a finite verb would have been expected here rather than this participle. He sees the participle as reflecting the flexibility of the Hebrew participle to act as a finite verb. If so, it is appropriate to translate this participle as if it were a finite verb [Moule, *Idiom Book*², 179]. Alternatively, it could be a concessive participle that is strengthened by καίπερ.)

7. πεποίθησιν: Case, case usage, word related to? [1+1+1]

_____

Philippians 3:5

8. περιτομῇ: Case, case usage, word related to? [1+1+1]

_____

9. κατά: Name the appropriate category for the use of this preposition here. What is the exegetical import of this use of κατά for this verse? (Consult *Basics* or *ExSyn* on prepositions.) [2+2]

_____

Philippians 3:6

10. τὴν ἐκκλησίαν: Case, case usage, word related to? [1+1+1]

_____

11. δικαιοσύνην: Case, case usage, word related to? [1+1+1]

_____

- τήν² (This article is substantiving the prepositional phrase ἐν νόμῳ, thus causing the phrase to be in apposition to δικαιοσύνην [cf. *ExSyn* 236; cf. *Basics* 105].)

Philippians 3:7

12. ταῦτα: Case, case usage, word related to? [1+1+1]

_____

13. ζημίαν: Case, case usage, word related to? [1+1+1]

_____

Philippians 3:8

14. μενοῦνγε: This is a rare emphatic conjunction. It is used in two other places in the New Testament (Rom 9:20 and 10:18). Give the appropriate gloss as found in BDAG for Phil 3:8. [2]

_____

15. πάντα: Case, case usage, word related to? [1+1+1]

_____

- εἶναι (The presence of εἶναι gives insight into understanding the semantics of the preceding verse [v. 7] as well as a clue as to how the accusatives surrounding εἶναι are to be classified. In the preceding verse ἡγέομαι is found with two accusatives. In this verse ἡγέομαι is again present but is used with εἶναι. This suggests a similar semantic meaning between the two although they are slightly different structurally [see *ExSyn* 182–89].)

16. ζημίαν: Case, case usage, word related to? [1+1+1]

_____

17. **τῆς γνώσεως**: Translate this word as an attributed genitive along with the word it modifies, τὸ ὑπερέχον. [4]

___

- **ἡγοῦμαι**[2] (The other two times ἡγέομαι [vv. 7, 8] is used in this section it has two accusatives with it. Here only σκύβαλα is present while τὰ πάντα is implied from the previous clause. Because Greek is an economical language, it is not necessary to repeat τὰ πάντα.)

18. **σκύβαλα**: Case, case usage, word related to? [1+1+2]

___

Philippians 3:9

19. **Χριστοῦ**: This could be taken as an objective genitive or a subjective genitive. Give a translation (with the preceding word) and explain the implications of each of these. [3+3]

___

___

Philippians 3:10

- **τοῦ γνῶναι** (This is an infinitive of purpose [cf. *Basics* 256-57; *ExSyn* 590-92].)

20. **αὐτόν**: Case, case usage, word related to? [1+1+1]

___

21. **κοινωνίαν**: Case, case usage, word related to? [1+1+1]

___

- **συμμορφιζόμενος** (This is a participle of means and can be rendered "by sharing [in his sufferings]" [cf. *Basics* 274-75; *ExSyn* 628-30].)

Philippians 1:9–13

Background

Paul begins this letter with his customary opening thanksgiving and prayer (1:3–11). First, he thanks God for the Philippians' participation in the gospel (1:3–5) and expresses confidence of their continued perseverance in the faith since God is at work in their hearts (1:6–8). Then he prays that they will grow in a discerning love (1:9–10), capping the prayer with an expression of confidence of their continued growth until the return of Christ (1:11). The apostle now turns to his own circumstances, which the Philippians had been desperate to learn about (1:12–26). Without so much as giving any details so as to invoke sympathy, Paul boldly states that his circumstances have advanced the gospel (1:12). He is evidently more concerned about the gospel than about his own life and thus begins to detail the effect that the gospel has had.

Text

1:9 Καὶ τοῦτο προσεύχομαι, ἵνα ἡ ἀγάπη ὑμῶν ἔτι μᾶλλον καὶ μᾶλλον περισσεύῃ ἐν ἐπιγνώσει καὶ πάσῃ αἰσθήσει **1:10** εἰς τὸ δοκιμάζειν ὑμᾶς τὰ διαφέροντα, ἵνα ἦτε εἰλικρινεῖς καὶ ἀπρόσκοποι εἰς ἡμέραν Χριστοῦ, **1:11** πεπληρωμένοι καρπὸν δικαιοσύνης τὸν διὰ Ἰησοῦ Χριστοῦ εἰς δόξαν καὶ ἔπαινον θεοῦ.

1:12 Γινώσκειν δὲ ὑμᾶς βούλομαι, ἀδελφοί, ὅτι τὰ κατ' ἐμὲ μᾶλλον εἰς προκοπὴν τοῦ εὐαγγελίου ἐλήλυθεν, **1:13** ὥστε τοὺς δεσμούς μου φανεροὺς ἐν Χριστῷ γενέσθαι ἐν ὅλῳ τῷ πραιτωρίῳ καὶ τοῖς λοιποῖς πᾶσιν.

Vocabulary

1. περισσεύω : I abound, surpass, overflow (v. 9)	8. ὁ ἔπαινος : praise, approval, recognition (v. 11)
2. ἡ ἐπίγνωσις : knowledge, recognition, consciousness (v. 9)	9. βούλομαι : I wish, want, desire (v. 12)
3. ἡ αἴσθησις : discernment, insight (v. 9)	10. ἡ προκοπή : progress, advancement (v. 12)
4. δοκιμάζω : I put to the test, examine (v. 10)	11. ὁ δεσμός : bond, fetter, chain (v. 13)
5. διαφέρω : I carry through; differ; things that really matter (as subst.) (v. 10)	12. φανερός : visible, clear, plainly to be seen (v. 13)
6. εἰλικρινής : pure, sincere (v. 10)	13. τὸ πραιτώριον : praetorium, imperial or palace guard (v. 13)
7. ἀπρόσκοπος : undamaged, blameless, clear (v. 10)	

Philippians 1:9

22. ἵνα ... περισσεύῃ: How exactly is this clause functioning? What is it related to? (cf. *Basics*, 206-7, *ExSyn* 471-76 [3+2])

_____

Philippians 1:10

- εἰς τὸ δοκιμάζειν (This infinitive is indicating purpose or possibly result [cf. *Basics* 256-57; *ExSyn* 590-92].)

23. ὑμᾶς: Case, case usage, word related to? How can you tell whether this is the subject or object of the infinitive δοκιμάζειν? [1+1+1+4]

_____

_____

24. τὰ διαφέροντα: Case, case usage, word related to? [1+1+1]

_____

Philippians 1:11

- πεπληρωμένοι (This participle is adverbial with either a causal or instrumental force. Most perfect adverbial participles are causal.)

25. καρπόν: Case, case usage, word related to? (Several witnesses have the genitive καρπῶν here [Ψ 1739ᶜ 1881 Byz].) If the genitive were the correct reading what would its case usage be? [1+1+1+2]

_____

_____

Philippians 1:12

26. ὅτι: Specific use of conjunction? Word related to? [2+1]

_____

- τά (This article is substantiving the prepositional phrase κατ' ἐμέ and causing the whole phrase to act as the subject of ἐλήλυθεν [cf. *Basics* 105; *ExSyn* 236].)

- κατ' (This preposition is "denoting a relationship to someth.," and should be rendered "with respect to" or "in relation to" [BDAG, s.v. κατά 6].)

Philippians 1:13

- ὥστε (This conjunction is communicating result [cf. *Basics* 301; *ExSyn* 677]. It is not unusual for an infinitive to follow this conjunction in this context.)

27. τοὺς δεσμούς: Case, case usage, word related to? [1+1+1]

_____

28. φανερούς: Case, case usage (treat as noun), word related to? [1+1+1]

_____

Lesson 5: Article (Part I)

You will need to read carefully the first chapter on the article (*Basics* 93–113; *ExSyn* 207–54) before working on this lesson. Pay careful attention to the kinds of questions being asked. Generally, they will be of two sorts: semantic or structural. If the question is asking about the semantic category of the article, consult *Basics* 97–103 or *ExSyn* 216–31. If the question is asking about the structural category, consult *Basics* 103–8 or *ExSyn* 231–43. Further, there are two kinds of structural categories: function markers and substantivers. Unless otherwise specified, the structural category for all non-nouns that take an article is "as a substantiver" and the structural category for all articular nouns is "function marker."

Warm-Up Passages

Vocabulary

1. τὸ γένημα : product, fruit, yield, harvest (Lk 22:18)	4. ἄρα : so, then, consequently (Ro 14:19)
2. ἡ ἄμπελος : vine, grapevine (Lk 22 :18)	5. διώκω : I persecute; pursue (Ro 14:19)
3. δυνατός : powerful, strong, mighty, able (Mk 9:23)	6. ἡ οἰκοδομή : building (up), construction, edification (Ro 14:19)

Luke 22:18

λέγω γὰρ ὑμῖν, ὅτι οὐ μὴ πίω ἀπὸ τοῦ νῦν ἀπὸ τοῦ γενήματος τῆς ἀμπέλου ἕως οὗ ἡ βασιλεία τοῦ θεοῦ ἔλθῃ.

1. **τοῦ νῦν**: Structural category? [4]

Mark 9:23

(Note that in v 22 a man has brought his son to Jesus, asking Jesus to cast out the demon from the boy. He pleads with Jesus as follows, "If you are able to do anything, help us by showing compassion on us" [εἴ τι δύνῃ, βοήθησον ἡμῖν σπλαγχνισθεὶς ἐφ᾽ ἡμᾶς].)

9:23 ὁ δὲ Ἰησοῦς εἶπεν αὐτῷ· τὸ εἰ δύνῃ, πάντα δυνατὰ τῷ πιστεύοντι.

2. **τὸ εἰ δύνῃ**: Structural Category? [4]

●Romans 14:19

Ἄρα οὖν τὰ τῆς εἰρήνης διώκωμεν καὶ τὰ τῆς οἰκοδομῆς τῆς εἰς ἀλλήλους.

3. τὰ τῆς εἰρήνης: Structural Category? [4]

_____

4. τῆς εἰς ἀλλήλους: Structural Category? [4]

_____

Syntax Passages

Ephesians 3:1–10

Background

To make sure that the Gentile audience did not see Paul as replacing the apostles, the author explains that his gospel is new in the sense that it was not revealed in the OT, but not in the sense that it was different in kind from that of the other apostles (3:1-7). Further, the content ●of the new spiritual community is now made explicit: Jew and Gentile are fellow heirs, fellow body-members, and fellow partakers of the promise (3:5-6). Jew and Gentile are thus on equal footing in this new body. Not only can these Gentiles not claim superiority to Jews (and vice versa), Paul himself cannot claim superiority to any Christian (3:8). But the Gentiles have been incorporated into the body of Christ not for their sake only, but even for the sake of angelic beings (3:10).

Text

3:1 Τούτου χάριν ἐγὼ Παῦλος ὁ δέσμιος τοῦ Χριστοῦ Ἰησοῦ ὑπὲρ ὑμῶν τῶν ἐθνῶν—**3:2** εἴ γε ἠκούσατε τὴν οἰκονομίαν τῆς χάριτος τοῦ θεοῦ τῆς δοθείσης μοι εἰς ὑμᾶς, **3:3** ὅτι κατὰ ἀποκάλυψιν ἐγνωρίσθη μοι τὸ μυστήριον, καθὼς προέγραψα ἐν ὀλίγῳ, **3:4** πρὸς ὃ δύνασθε ἀναγινώσκοντες νοῆσαι τὴν σύνεσίν μου ἐν τῷ μυστηρίῳ τοῦ Χριστοῦ, **3:5** ὃ ἑτέραις γενεαῖς οὐκ ἐγνωρίσθη τοῖς υἱοῖς τῶν ἀνθρώπων ὡς νῦν ἀπεκαλύφθη τοῖς ἁγίοις ἀποστόλοις αὐτοῦ καὶ προφήταις ἐν πνεύματι, **3:6** εἶναι τὰ ἔθνη συγκληρονόμα καὶ σύσσωμα καὶ συμμέτοχα τῆς ἐπαγγελίας ἐν Χριστῷ Ἰησοῦ διὰ τοῦ εὐαγγελίου, **3:7** οὗ ἐγενήθην διάκονος κατὰ τὴν δωρεὰν τῆς χάριτος τοῦ θεοῦ τῆς δοθείσης μοι κατὰ τὴν ἐνέργειαν τῆς δυνάμεως αὐτοῦ.

3:8 Ἐμοὶ τῷ ἐλαχιστοτέρῳ πάντων ἁγίων ἐδόθη ἡ χάρις αὕτη, τοῖς ἔθνεσιν εὐαγγελίσασθαι τὸ ἀνεξιχνίαστον πλοῦτος τοῦ Χριστοῦ **3:9** καὶ φωτίσαι πάντας τίς ἡ οἰκονομία τοῦ μυστηρίου τοῦ ἀποκεκρυμμένου ἀπὸ τῶν αἰώνων ἐν τῷ θεῷ τῷ τὰ πάντα κτίσαντι, **3:10** ἵνα γνωρισθῇ νῦν ταῖς ἀρχαῖς καὶ ταῖς ἐξουσίαις ἐν τοῖς ἐπουρανίοις διὰ τῆς ἐκκλησίας ἡ πολυποίκιλος σοφία τοῦ θεοῦ.

Vocabulary

1. χάριν : on account of, for the sake of (v. 1)	15. συγκληρονόμος : co-heir (subst. in NT) (v. 6)
2. ὁ δέσμιος : prisoner (v. 1)	16. σύσσωμος : fellow-members (as subst.) (v. 6)
3. γέ : at least, even, indeed, yet (v. 2)	17. συμμέτοχος : sharing with; sharer (v. 6)
4. ἡ οἰκονομία : arrangement, order, plan, management (of a household) (v. 2)	18. ὁ διάκονος : servant, minister (v. 7)
5. ἡ ἀποκάλυψις : revelation, disclosure (v. 3)	19. ἡ δωρεά : gift, bounty (v. 7)
6. γνωρίζω : I make known, reveal (v. 3)	20. ἡ ἐνέργεια : working, operation (v. 7)
7. τὸ μυστήριον : (God's) secret, mystery (v. 3)	21. ἐλάχιστος : least, smallest, unimportant (v. 8)
8. προγράφω : I write before or above, write in earlier times (v. 3)	22. ἀνεξιχνίαστος : inscrutable, incomprehensible (v. 8)
9. ὀλίγος : few, little, small; briefly (v. 3)	23. ὁ, τὸ πλοῦτος : riches, wealth, abundance (v. 8)
10. ἀναγινώσκω : I read (v. 4)	24. φωτίζω : enlighten; I shine, give light to, illuminate (v. 9)
11. νοέω : I perceive, apprehend, understand (v. 4)	25. ἀποκρύπτω : I hide, keep secret (v. 9)
12. ἡ σύνεσις : intelligence, acuteness, insight (v. 4)	26. κτίζω : I create, make (v. 9)
13. ἡ γενεά : race, kind; generation (v. 5)	27. ἐπουράνιος : celestial, heavenly (v. 10)
14. ἀποκαλύπτω : I reveal, disclose (v. 5)	28. πολυποίκιλος : (very) many-sided (v. 10)

Ephesians 3:1

- **χάριν** (This is the accusative of χάρις; as such, it functions as a preposition. BDAG notes that this "preposition" is "almost always after the word it governs" [BDAG, s.v. χάριν]. In this case it governs τούτου and can be rendered, with τούτου, "for this reason.")

5. **ὁ δέσμιος:** Semantic category? [4]

- **Ἰησοῦ** (Several early and important witnesses, chiefly of the Western text, lack Ἰησοῦ here, while most Alexandrian and Byzantine MSS have the word. Normally, we would not expect scribes to intentionally omit the name of Jesus but would expect them to add it. However, because of the Western text's proclivities to delete or add to the text, seemingly at whim, serious doubts should be attached to the shorter reading. It is strengthened, however, by ℵ's support (ℵ, or Sinaiticus, is one of the most important Alexandrian MSS). But this needs to be balanced off by the fact that ℵ was corrected early on with the addition of Ἰησοῦ, and by the fact that D, a leading Western MS, was also corrected in the same direction. Whether Ἰησοῦ was original is a difficult decision, but the probability that it was is a bit stronger than otherwise.)

- τῶν ἐθνῶν (Here is a good example of the article used with a generic noun. "The Gentiles" refers to Gentiles as a class, not a specific group of Gentiles in a given location. Even though "you Gentiles" is what the author says, he is not limiting his ministry to those in Asia Minor.)

Ephesians 3:2

- εἴ γε (The particle γε is an intensifier and in connection with εἰ should be rendered "if indeed.")

6. τὴν οἰκονομίαν: Often the semantic category of an article is affected by whether or not the modifiers associated with it are in view. Modifiers make the article progress from general to more specific. What is the semantic category of this article if the whole phrase is in view [τὴν οἰκονομίαν τῆς χάριτος τοῦ θεοῦ τῆς δοθείσης μοι]? [4]

_____

7. τῆς δοθείσης: Structural category? [3]

_____

Ephesians 3:3

8. τὸ μυστήριον: Read Ephesians 1:9–11 in English. In light of that text, what might be the semantic category of this article? [3]

_____

Ephesians 3:4

- ἀναγινώσκοντες (This is an adverbial participle related to δύνασθε. The action of the participle is "contemporaneous in time to the action of the main verb" [*ExSyn* 625; cf. *Basics* 273; *ExSyn* 625–27]. If it is a simple temporal participle, it can be rendered "[which you will be able to understand] while reading." If it is a participle of means, it can be rendered "[which you will be able to understand] by reading.")

9. **τὴν σύνεσιν**: Structural category? [3]

_____

10. **τῷ μυστηρίῳ**: Semantic category? [3]

_____

Ephesians 3:5

- **τοῖς υἱοῖς** (BDAG notes that this phrase refers to "the individual members of a large and coherent group," and that "the sons of men = humans" [BDAG, s.v. υἱός 2.b].)

11. **τοῖς ἁγίοις ἀποστόλοις**: What is the semantic category of this article if the whole phrase is in view (τοῖς ἁγίοις ἀποστόλοις αὐτοῦ καὶ προφήταις)? [3]

_____

Ephesians 3:6

- **εἶναι** (This is an appositional infinitive that defines the noun it is related to. In this case it is defining the content of the "mystery" from 3:4 [cf. _Basics_ 262–63; _ExSyn_ 606–7].)

12. **τὰ ἔθνη**: Structural category? [4]

_____

13. **τῆς ἐπαγγελίας**: If ἐν Χριστῷ modifies ἐπαγγελίας, what is the semantic category of this article? If τῆς ἐπαγγελίας is taken by itself without any modifiers, what is the semantic category of this article? [2+2]

_____

14. **τοῦ εὐαγγελίου**: Semantic category? (One important factor to remember with the word εὐαγγέλιον is that it did not simply mean "gospel" in the specific sense in which it is sometimes thought of today. It had a broader meaning in the Greco-Roman world. Note, for example, what Friedrich says in the _TDNT_ [2:724] about the "εὐαγγέλιον in the imperial cult. This is the most important usage for our purpose. Note must be taken of what is said concerning the θεῖος ἄνθρωπος … τύχη and σωτηρία. The emperor unites all these in his own person. This is what gives εὐαγγέλιον its significance and power. The ruler is divine by nature. His power extends to men, to animals, to the earth and to the

LESSON 5: ARTICLE (PART I)   57

sea. Nature belongs to him; wind and waves are subject to him. He works miracles and heals men. He is the saviour of the world who also redeems individuals from their difficulties.... He has appeared on earth as a deity in human form." In the Pauline letters, εὐαγγέλιον is used more often than in the rest of the NT combined. There may be a hint in them that the author is contrasting the εὐαγγέλιον about Caesar with the εὐαγγέλιον about Jesus Christ.) [2]

Ephesians 3:7

15 τὴν δωρεάν: If you read the entire phrase τὴν δωρεὰν τῆς χάριτος τοῦ θεοῦ τῆς δοθείσης μοι as a whole, how should τήν be taken semantically? [3]

---

16. τῆς χάριτος: Structural category? [3]

---

17. τοῦ θεοῦ: Structural category? [2]

---

18. τῆς δοθείσης: Structural category? [2]

Ephesians 3:8

* τῷ ἐλαχιστοτέρῳ (BDF notes that this is a "new formation" [BDF §61.2]. The author has apparently coined a phrase to highlight the humility of Paul's self-assessment. This form is actually the comparative of a superlative. Normally translated, "less than the least," the vernacular "leaster" captures what the author has done.)

19. πάντων ἁγίων: Case, case usage, word related to? (Treat both words together as a unit.) [1+2+1]

---

20. ἡ χάρις: Structural category? [3]

_____

21. τοῖς ἔθνεσιν: Semantic category? [3]

_____

22. τὸ ἀνεξιχνίαστον πλοῦτος: Semantic category? [3]

_____

Ephesians 3:9

- **πάντας** (Several important MSS include πάντας [P⁴⁶ ² B C D F G Ψ 33 Byz latt sy co]. On the other hand, there are also a few important MSS that exlude this reading [א A 0150 1739]. Metzger notes the possibility of an intentional omission since πάντας conflicts with ἔθνεσιν in 3:8 [*Textual Commentary*², 534]. But it is also possible to explain its inclusion in that an accusative would be expected with φωτίσαι. Given the multiple possiblities it is difficult to decide which reading is original. In such instances, it is best to follow the external evidence.)

- **τίς ἡ οἰκονομία** (This interrogative pronoun is not used in a direct question here, but an indirect. If you translate it "as to what is the plan ..." it should make sense.)

23. ἡ οἰκονομία: Semantic category? (See v. 2 for help.) [4]

_____

24. τῷ ... κτίσαντι: Structural category? [3]

_____

Ephesians 3:10

25. ταῖς ἀρχαῖς: Semantic category? (See BDAG on ἀρχή for help.) [3]

_____

26. τοῖς ἐπουρανίοις: Structural category? [3]

_____

27. τῆς ἐκκλησίας: Semantic category? (See BDAG for help.) [2]

_____

28. ἡ πολυποίκιλος σοφία: Semantic category? [3]

_____

John 4:39–43

Background

After spending some time in Jerusalem, Jesus traveled back to Galilee, going through Samaria en route (4:1–42). Here we see the account of Jesus' conversation with and conversion of the woman at the well. In Samaria, Jesus performed no "sign," although he did prove himself to be a prophet. Yet, the citizens of Sychar embraced him as "the Savior of the world" (4:42).

Text

4:39 Ἐκ δὲ τῆς πόλεως ἐκείνης πολλοὶ ἐπίστευσαν εἰς αὐτὸν τῶν Σαμαριτῶν διὰ τὸν λόγον τῆς γυναικὸς μαρτυρούσης ὅτι εἶπέν μοι πάντα ἃ ἐποίησα. **4:40** ὡς οὖν ἦλθον πρὸς αὐτὸν οἱ Σαμαρῖται, ἠρώτων αὐτὸν μεῖναι παρ' αὐτοῖς· καὶ ἔμεινεν ἐκεῖ δύο ἡμέρας. **4:41** καὶ πολλῷ πλείους ἐπίστευσαν διὰ τὸν λόγον αὐτοῦ, **4:42** τῇ τε γυναικὶ ἔλεγον ὅτι οὐκέτι διὰ τὴν σὴν λαλιὰν πιστεύομεν, αὐτοὶ γὰρ ἀκηκόαμεν καὶ οἴδαμεν ὅτι οὗτός ἐστιν ἀληθῶς ὁ σωτὴρ τοῦ κόσμου.
4:43 Μετὰ δὲ τὰς δύο ἡμέρας ἐξῆλθεν ἐκεῖθεν εἰς τὴν Γαλιλαίαν.

Vocabulary

1. ὁ Σαμαρίτης : a Samaritan (v. 39)	5. ἡ λαλιά : speech, speaking (v. 42)
2. πλείους : nom. pl. m. of πλείων more (v. 41)	6. ἀληθῶς : truly, in truth, really, actually (v. 42)
3. οὐκέτι : no longer, no more (v. 42)	7. ὁ σωτήρ : Savior, deliverer, preserver (v. 42)
4. σός : your (v. 42)	

John 4:39

29. τῆς πόλεως: Structural category? [2]

_____

- τῶν Σαμαριτῶν (This genitive modifies πολλοί although it is separated by several words.)

- τῆς γυναικὸς μαρτυρούσης (By structure the participle is in predicate position to the noun, yet virtually all translations treat it as an attributive participle. If it is an adjectival participle, the words can be translated "the woman who testified"; if it is an adverbial participle, it can be translated "the woman when she testified.")

John 4:40

30. οἱ Σαμαρῖται: Semantic category? [2]

_____

John 4:41

- πολλῷ πλείους (Although most translations render this as "many more," it could also be translated "the many by much" or "the many much more." At issue is whether more Samaritans are in view or whether the majority of the Samaritans in this town who already believed now believe more deeply. Their response to the woman in v. 42 ["no longer do we believe because of your testimony"] suggests that the latter translation is to be preferred, since οὐκέτι seems to imply prior belief.)

31. τὸν λόγον: Structural category? [2]

_____

John 4:42

32. τῇ τε γυναικί: Semantic category? [2]

_____

- τέ (The use of τέ without a subsequent καί or τέ is rare in the New Testament and is confined mostly to Acts and a few other places [cf. Matt 28:12; Luke 24:20; John 6:18; Rom 2:19; 16:26; Eph 3:19; Heb 1:3; 12:2; and Jude 6]. It functions like a connective conjunction, but as Robertson notes, "it seems certain that τέ indicates a somewhat closer unity than does καί" [Robertson, _Grammar_ 1178]. The close connection can be seen in this context in that John 4:42 is the result of John 4:41.)

33. ὁ σωτήρ: This is another example where the modifier can affect the interpretation. What is the semantic category of the article if τοῦ κόσμου is included? What if ὁ σωτήρ is read alone? [2+2]

_____

_____

34. τὰς δύο ἡμέρας: Semantic category? [3]

_____

Lesson 6: Article (Part II)

You will need to read carefully the first chapter on the article (*Basics* 93-113; *ExSyn* 207-54) before working on this lesson. Pay careful attention to the kind of question being asked. Generally, they will be of two sorts: semantic or structural. If the question is asking about the semantic category of the article, consult *Basics* 97-103 or *ExSyn* 216-31. If the question is asking about the structural category, consult *Basics* 103-8 or *ExSyn* 231-43.

Furthermore, there are two kinds of structural categories: function markers and substantivers. Unless otherwise specified, the structural category for all non-nouns that take an article is "as a substantiver" and the structural category for all articular nouns is "function marker." In addition, some of the questions in this lesson ask about anarthrous substantives. These will be in the form "Explain the absence of the article," "anarthrous category?" or the like. For these questions, see *Basics* 108-13 or *ExSyn* 243-54.

Syntax Passages

John 4:43-54

Background

After spending time in Samaria, Jesus returns to Galilee, where a second sign is performed, the healing of a royal official's son (John 4:43-54). Yet the sign is performed within the context of the Galileans hearing about his feats in Jerusalem. Hence, there is misunderstanding on their part in that, once again, they only want Jesus as Healer (4:48), not as Savior.

Text

4:43 Μετὰ δὲ τὰς δύο ἡμέρας ἐξῆλθεν ἐκεῖθεν εἰς τὴν Γαλιλαίαν· **4:44** αὐτὸς γὰρ Ἰησοῦς ἐμαρτύρησεν ὅτι προφήτης ἐν τῇ ἰδίᾳ πατρίδι τιμὴν οὐκ ἔχει. **4:45** ὅτε οὖν ἦλθεν εἰς τὴν Γαλιλαίαν, ἐδέξαντο αὐτὸν οἱ Γαλιλαῖοι πάντα ἑωρακότες ὅσα ἐποίησεν ἐν Ἱεροσολύμοις ἐν τῇ ἑορτῇ, καὶ αὐτοὶ γὰρ ἦλθον εἰς τὴν ἑορτήν.

4:46 Ἦλθεν οὖν πάλιν εἰς τὴν Κανὰ τῆς Γαλιλαίας, ὅπου ἐποίησεν τὸ ὕδωρ οἶνον. Καὶ ἦν τις βασιλικὸς οὗ ὁ υἱὸς ἠσθένει ἐν Καφαρναούμ. **4:47** οὗτος ἀκούσας ὅτι Ἰησοῦς ἥκει ἐκ τῆς Ἰουδαίας εἰς τὴν Γαλιλαίαν ἀπῆλθεν πρὸς αὐτὸν καὶ ἠρώτα ἵνα καταβῇ καὶ ἰάσηται αὐτοῦ τὸν υἱόν, ἤμελλεν γὰρ ἀποθνῄσκειν. **4:48** εἶπεν οὖν ὁ Ἰησοῦς πρὸς αὐτόν· ἐὰν μὴ σημεῖα καὶ τέρατα ἴδητε, οὐ μὴ πιστεύσητε. **4:49** λέγει πρὸς αὐτὸν ὁ βασιλικός· κύριε, κατάβηθι πρὶν ἀποθανεῖν τὸ παιδίον μου. **4:50** λέγει αὐτῷ ὁ Ἰησοῦς· πορεύου· ὁ υἱός σου ζῇ. ἐπίστευσεν ὁ ἄνθρωπος τῷ λόγῳ ὃν εἶπεν αὐτῷ ὁ Ἰησοῦς καὶ ἐπορεύετο. **4:51** ἤδη δὲ αὐτοῦ καταβαίνοντος οἱ δοῦλοι αὐτοῦ ὑπήντησαν αὐτῷ λέγοντες ὅτι ὁ παῖς αὐτοῦ ζῇ. **4:52** ἐπύθετο οὖν τὴν ὥραν παρ' αὐτῶν ἐν ᾗ κομψότερον ἔσχεν· εἶπαν οὖν αὐτῷ ὅτι ἐχθὲς ὥραν ἑβδόμην ἀφῆκεν αὐτὸν ὁ πυρετός. **4:53** ἔγνω οὖν ὁ πατὴρ ὅτι ἐν ἐκείνῃ τῇ ὥρᾳ ἐν ᾗ εἶπεν αὐτῷ ὁ Ἰησοῦς· ὁ υἱός σου ζῇ, καὶ ἐπίστευσεν αὐτὸς καὶ ἡ οἰκία αὐτοῦ ὅλη. **4:54** Τοῦτο δὲ πάλιν δεύτερον σημεῖον ἐποίησεν ὁ Ἰησοῦς ἐλθὼν ἐκ τῆς Ἰουδαίας εἰς τὴν Γαλιλαίαν.

Vocabulary

1. ἐκεῖθεν : from there (v. 43)	13. ἰάομαι : I heal, cure; restore (v. 47)
2. ἡ πατρίς : fatherland; home town (v. 44)	14. τὸ τέρας : prodigy, wonder, omen (v. 48)
3. ἡ τιμή : value, honor, respect (v. 44)	15. πρίν : before (v. 49)
4. Γαλιλαῖος : Galilean (v. 45)	16. ὑπαντάω : I meet; encounter, oppose (v. 51)
5. ἡ ἑορτή : festival, celebration (v. 45)	17. ὁ, ἡ παῖς : masc. boy, youth; fem. daughter, girl (v. 51)
6. ἡ Κανά : Cana (v. 46)	18. πυνθάνομαι : I inquire, ask; learn (v. 52)
7. ὁ οἶνος : wine, vineyard (v. 46)	19. κομψότερον : better (v. 52)
8. ὁ βασιλικός : royal; royal official (v. 46)	20. ἐχθές : yesterday (v. 52)
9. ἀσθενέω : I am weak, sick, powerless (v. 46)	21. ἕβδομος : seventh (v. 52)
10. ἡ Καφαρναούμ : Capernaum (v. 46)	22. ἡ πυρετός : fever (v. 52)
11. ἥκω : I have come, am present (v. 47)	23. δεύτερος : second (v. 54)
12. Ἰουδαία : Judea (v. 47)	

John 4:43

1. **τὰς δύο ἡμέρας**: Semantic category? [2]

John 4:44

- **Ἰησοῦς** (If this were a question about the anarthrous noun, it would be: Why is the article absent — i.e., what is the anarthrous category? The three general choices are indefinite, qualitative, or definite. The appropriate answer is that this noun is definite. The specific reason should also be given: it is a proper name. It can be stated as follows: Definite; proper name.)

2. **προφήτης**: Explain the absence of the article. [2]

- τιμήν (The anarthrous category for this noun is qualitative. It is an abstract noun and, as such, focuses on quality.)

John 4:45

- ἑωρακότες (This is a participle of cause related to ἐδέξαντο. It can be rendered "[all the Galileans received him] because they had seen . . ." [cf. *Basics* 275-76; *ExSyn* 631-32].)

3. Ἱεροσολύμοις: Explain the absence of the article. [2]

_____

- ἐν τῇ ἑορτῇ (ἐν here has a temporal force, "during.")

4. τῇ ἑορτῇ: Semantic category? (See BDAG on ἑορτή for help.) [4]

_____

John 4:46

5. τὴν Κανά: Structural category? Some MSS lack the article here. Although the article with indeclinable nouns is often used to clarify what case the noun is in, would the lack of it in some MSS make the case difficult to discern? [2+2]

_____

_____

6. τὸ ὕδωρ: Structural category? [3]

_____

7. οἶνον: Case, case usage, word related to? [1+2+1]

_____

8. βασιλικός: Explain the absence of the article. [2]

_____

9. Καφαρναούμ: Explain the absence of the article. [2]

_____

● John 4:47

- ἀκούσας (This is a temporal participle of antecedent or possibly contemporaneous time modifying ἀπῆλθεν. It can be rendered "after he heard" or "when he heard" [cf. *Basics* 272-73; *ExSyn* 623-27].)

10. Ἰησοῦς: Anarthrous category? [2]

_____

John 4:49

- πρὶν ἀποθανεῖν (This is an infinitive of subsequent time modifying κατάβηθι. It can be rendered, "before [my child] dies" [cf. *Basics* 258-59; *ExSyn* 594-96].)

John 4:50

11. ὁ ἄνθρωπος: Semantic category? What is the antecedent? [2+2]

●

_____

John 4:51

- καταβαίνοντος (This is a genitive absolute participle, which functions like a subordinate adverbial clause. Here it can be rendered, "while [he] was going down" [cf. *Basics* 284; *ExSyn* 654-55].)

- παῖς αὐτοῦ (There are several variants for this verse. The best MSS read παῖς αὐτοῦ [P66*, 75 ℵ A B C], while others have different variations, either exchanging υἱός for παῖς or σου for αὐτοῦ. If παῖς αὐτοῦ is seen as the original reading, then the other variants can be explained. First, this is the only place in John where παῖς is used; thus scribes would be tempted to make this verse conform to the earlier sections [vv. 46, 47, 50, and 53]. Also, the σου can be explained since "ὅτι was taken by some copyists to be ὅτι *recitativum*, introducing the actual words of the servants" [Metzger, *Textual Commentary*[2], 178].)

John 4:52

- κομψότερον ἔσχεν (BDAG states that this phrase is idiomatic and can be rendered "begin to improve" [BDAG, s.v. κομψότερον].)

●

12. ὥραν ἑβδόμην: Explain the absence of the article. [2]

_____

13. ὁ πυρετός: Semantic category? [4]

_____

John 4:53

14. ὁ πατήρ: Semantic category? List all the noun antecedents with their verses. [2+3]

_____

John 4:54

15. Τοῦτο: Case, case usage, word related to? Most modern translations render the clause that this pronoun is in as, "This was the second sign that Jesus did...." Assuming that such translations are intended to reflect the structure of the Greek, what have they done incorrectly here? How does a proper understanding of the construction impact the exegesis of the verse? [1+3+1; 2; 2]

_____

_____

_____

16. σημεῖον: Case, case usage, word related to? [2+2+2]

_____

• ἐλθών (This is a temporal participle of antecedent or contemporaneous time modifying ἐποίησεν. It can be rendered "after he came" or "when he came" [cf. *Basics* 272–73; *ExSyn* 623–27].)

Luke 1:26–40

Background

   At the beginning of the Gospel of Luke, two births are prophesied (1:5–56), John the Baptist's (1:5–25) and Jesus' (1:26–38). There are many parallels between these two pericopae (e.g., announcement by an angel [1:11-17; 1:29-33], disbelief or doubt on the part of the recipient [1:18-22; 1:34-37], and response on the part of the mother-to-be [1:23-25; 1:38]). But there are three significant differences: (1) the angel comes to the father-to-be of John, while he comes to the mother-to-be of Jesus, and (2) though both births will be miraculous, the birth of Jesus is unique, for he is conceived by a virgin; (3) Zechariah's questioning is met with the discipline of dumbness, while Mary's question is answered positively. Whatever else this tells us, Jesus is already seen to be more significant than his forerunner. Mary then visits Elizabeth (1:39-56), where a foreshadowing of Jesus' greatness is seen in that the baby in Elizabeth's womb leaps for joy (1:40, 42) and she exclaims to Mary, "Blessed are you among women!" (1:42).

Text

1:26 Ἐν δὲ τῷ μηνὶ τῷ ἕκτῳ ἀπεστάλη ὁ ἄγγελος Γαβριὴλ ἀπὸ τοῦ θεοῦ εἰς πόλιν τῆς Γαλιλαίας ᾗ ὄνομα Ναζαρὲθ **1:27** πρὸς παρθένον ἐμνηστευμένην ἀνδρὶ ᾧ ὄνομα Ἰωσὴφ ἐξ οἴκου Δαυὶδ καὶ τὸ ὄνομα τῆς παρθένου Μαριάμ. **1:28** καὶ εἰσελθὼν πρὸς αὐτὴν εἶπεν· χαῖρε, κεχαριτωμένη, ὁ κύριος μετὰ σοῦ. **1:29** ἡ δὲ ἐπὶ τῷ λόγῳ διεταράχθη καὶ διελογίζετο ποταπὸς εἴη ὁ ἀσπασμὸς οὗτος. **1:30** καὶ εἶπεν ὁ ἄγγελος αὐτῇ·

> Μὴ φοβοῦ, Μαριάμ, εὗρες γὰρ χάριν παρὰ τῷ θεῷ.
> **1:31** καὶ ἰδοὺ συλλήμψῃ ἐν γαστρὶ καὶ τέξῃ υἱόν
> καὶ καλέσεις τὸ ὄνομα αὐτοῦ Ἰησοῦν.
> **1:32** οὗτος ἔσται μέγας καὶ υἱὸς ὑψίστου κληθήσεται
> καὶ δώσει αὐτῷ κύριος ὁ θεὸς τὸν θρόνον Δαυὶδ τοῦ πατρὸς αὐτοῦ,
> **1:33** καὶ βασιλεύσει ἐπὶ τὸν οἶκον Ἰακὼβ εἰς τοὺς αἰῶνας
> καὶ τῆς βασιλείας αὐτοῦ οὐκ ἔσται τέλος.

1:34 εἶπεν δὲ Μαριὰμ πρὸς τὸν ἄγγελον, Πῶς ἔσται τοῦτο, ἐπεὶ ἄνδρα οὐ γινώσκω; **1:35** καὶ ἀποκριθεὶς ὁ ἄγγελος εἶπεν αὐτῇ·

> πνεῦμα ἅγιον ἐπελεύσεται ἐπὶ σὲ
> καὶ δύναμις ὑψίστου ἐπισκιάσει σοι·
> διὸ καὶ τὸ γεννώμενον ἅγιον κληθήσεται υἱὸς θεοῦ.

1:36 καὶ ἰδοὺ Ἐλισάβετ ἡ συγγενίς σου καὶ αὐτὴ συνείληφεν υἱὸν ἐν γήρει αὐτῆς καὶ οὗτος μὴν ἕκτος ἐστὶν αὐτῇ τῇ καλουμένῃ στείρᾳ· **1:37** ὅτι οὐκ ἀδυνατήσει παρὰ τοῦ θεοῦ πᾶν ῥῆμα. **1:38** εἶπεν δὲ Μαριάμ· ἰδοὺ ἡ δούλη κυρίου· γένοιτό μοι κατὰ τὸ ῥῆμά σου. καὶ ἀπῆλθεν ἀπ᾽ αὐτῆς ὁ ἄγγελος.

1:39 Ἀναστᾶσα δὲ Μαριὰμ ἐν ταῖς ἡμέραις ταύταις ἐπορεύθη εἰς τὴν ὀρεινὴν μετὰ σπουδῆς εἰς πόλιν Ἰούδα, **1:40** καὶ εἰσῆλθεν εἰς τὸν οἶκον Ζαχαρίου καὶ ἠσπάσατο τὴν Ἐλισάβετ.

Vocabulary

1. ὁ μήν : month, new moon (v. 26)	19. ὕψιστος : highest; the Most High (as subst.) (v. 32)
2. ἕκτος : sixth (v. 26)	20. βασιλεύω : I am king, I rule, reign (v. 33)
3. ὁ Γαβριήλ : Gabriel (v. 26)	21. ὁ Ἰακώβ : Jacob (v. 33)
4. ἡ Ναζαρέθ : Nazareth (v. 26)	22. τὸ τέλος : end, termination; close (v. 33)
5. ὁ, ἡ παρθένος : virgin (v. 27)	23. ἐπεί : because, since, for, then (v. 34)
6. μνηστεύω : I betroth; become engaged (pass in NT) (v. 27)	24. ἐπέρχομαι : I come, arrive; happen (v. 35)
7. ὁ Ἰωσήφ : Joseph (v. 27)	25. ἐπισκιάζω : I overshadow; cover (v. 35)
8. ἡ Μαριάμ : Mary (v. 27)	26. ἡ Ἐλισάβετ : Elizabeth (v. 36)
9. χαῖρε : hail, welcome (fr. χαίρω) (v. 28)	27. ἡ συγγενίς : kinswoman, relative (v. 36)
10. χαριτόω : I bless; favored one (as subst.) (v. 28)	28. τὸ γῆρας : old age (v. 36)
11. διαταράσσω : I am confused, greatly perplexed (pass in NT) (v. 29)	29. ἡ στεῖρα : barren woman (v. 36)
12. διαλογίζομαι : I consider, ponder, reason (v. 29)	30. ἀδυνατέω : I am powerless; it is impossible (impers. in NT) (v. 37)
13. ποταπός : of what sort or kind (?), how great? (v. 29)	31. ἡ δούλη : female slave (v. 38)
14. εἴη : pres. opt. of εἰμί (v. 29)	32. ὀρεινός : mountainous; hill country (as subst.) (v. 39)
15. ὁ ἀσπασμός : greeting (v. 29)	33. ἡ σπουδή : haste, speed; zeal, eagerness (v. 39)
16. συλλαμβάνω : I become pregnant, conceive (v. 31)	34. ὁ Ἰούδας : Judah, Judas (v. 39)
17. ἡ γαστήρ : belly, glutton; womb (v. 31)	35. ὁ Ζαχαρίας : Zachariah (v. 40)
18. τίκτω : I give birth (to), bear (v. 31)	

Luke 1:26

- Ἐν δὲ τῷ μηνὶ τῷ ἕκτῳ (This phrase should be rendered "in the sixth month." The sixth month of Elizabeth's pregnancy is in view.)

17. πόλιν: Objects of prepositions are routinely definite; the article is not needed to make them so. However objects of prepositions can also be qualitative or indefinite. Which of these three is it here, and why? Defend your answer in one or two sentences. [3+5]

_____

_____

_____

Luke 1:27

18. Δαυίδ: Explain the absence of the article. [2]

_____

Luke 1:28

- σοῦ (Several MSS add εὐλογημένη σύ ἐν γυναιξίν [or variations of this] to this reading. This seems to be a scribal addition to conform to 1:42, where these words are stated explicitly [Metzger, *Textual Commentary*[2], 108].)

Luke 1:29

19. ἡ: Which pronoun is this article functioning in the place of? [4]

_____

20. τῷ λόγῳ: Semantic category? What is the antecedent? [2+2]

_____

- διελογίζετο (This is an ingressive imperfect. It is used "to stress the beginning of an action, with the implication that it continued for some time" [*ExSyn* 544; cf. *Basics* 233-34; *ExSyn* 544-45]. Ingressive imperfects involve "the close collocation of two verbs denoting sequenced situations such that the first indicates the beginning-point of the second" [Fanning, *Verbal Aspect* 191-92]. Here the verb διεταράχθη creates a beginning point for διελογίζετο. Thus the imposition of a beginning point for a progressive aspect creates an ingressive idea. After Mary "was troubled," she "began to wonder.")

- εἴη (This is an oblique optative. Occasionally, the optative is "used in indirect questions after a secondary tense (i.e., one that takes the augment—aorist, imperfect, pluperfect). The optative substitutes for an indicative or subjunctive of the direct question. This occurs about a dozen times, depending on textual variants, but only in Luke's writings" [*ExSyn* 483].)

21. ὁ ἀσπασμός: Semantic category? [2]

_____

Luke 1:30

- Μαριάμ (This indeclinable noun is obviously definite since it is a proper name. The lack of the article could also possibly be explained if it is taken as a vocative, since vocatives cannot take the article.)

22. χάριν: Anarthrous category? [2]

_____

Luke 1:31

23. υἱόν: Explain the absence of the article. [2]

_____

- Ἰησοῦν (The reason this is anarthrous can be variously explained. Certainly it is a definite noun, since it is a proper name. But it may also be anarthrous since it is the complement in an object-complement construction. One of the ways to tell which is the object in such constructions is that the object will have the article, will be a proper name, or will be a pronoun. But when the complement is one of these, then word order seems to be decisive.)

Luke 1:32

24. υἱός: Explain the absence of the article. [2]

_____

LESSON 6: ARTICLE (PART II)   71

Luke 1:33

25. Ἰακώβ: Case, case usage, word related to? [1+1+1]

_____

Luke 1:34

26. ἄνδρα: Anarthrous category? [2]

_____

Luke 1:35

27. πνεῦμα: Explain the absence of the article. Keep in mind that the adjective ἅγιον is modifying πνεῦμα. [2]

_____

28. δύναμις: Anarthrous category? [2]

_____

29. τὸ γεννώμενον: Structural category? [4]

_____

- τὸ γεννώμενον (Some MSS add ἐκ σοῦ after τὸ γεννώμενον. The best witnesses exclude it [א B L W]. This is most likely a scribal addition for sake of clarity.)

Luke 1:36

30. υἱόν: Anarthrous category? [2]

_____

31. γήρει: Explain the absence of the article. [2]

_____

32. μὴν ἕκτος: Explain the absence of the article. [2]

- αὐτῇ τῇ καλουμένῃ στείρᾳ (This construction can be translated "for her who is called barren." The idea of the larger construction is that "this is the sixth month [of pregnancy] for her who is called barren." The dative αὐτῇ is a dative of reference; the participle τῇ καλουμένῃ is adjectival but also has a verbal element; the adjective στείρᾳ is a predicate adjective linked to αὐτῇ by the passive participle which is functioning like an equative verb.)

Luke 1:37

- ῥῆμα (Normally, ῥῆμα refers to a word or saying, but here it refers to a "thing," "object," or "matter" [BDAG, s.v. ῥῆμα 2]. It is functioning as the subject of ἀδυνατήσει and can be rendered, with οὐκ ... πᾶν "nothing [will be impossible for God].")

33. ῥῆμα: Explain the absence of the article. [2]

Luke 1:38

- ἡ δούλη κυρίου (The lack of the article before κυρίου is due to the fact that κυρίου here represents YHWH. In Hebrew, YHWH cannot take the article. The Greek of the LXX and NT sometimes retains the Hebrew idiom [i.e., an anarthrous YHWH] even though such a construction would be a violation of Apollonius' Canon. κυρίου thus is definite and the whole phrase can be translated "the servant of the Lord.")

- γένοιτο (This is a voluntative optative and is used to express an "obtainable wish" [ExSyn 481; cf. Basics 209-10; ExSyn 481-83].)

Luke 1:39

34. Ἰούδα: Anarthrous category? [2]

Lesson 7: Adjective

The questions on the adjective in this lesson will be one of two types: either adjectival *usage* or adjectival *position*. If adjectival usage is asked, you will need to consult *Basics* 129-35 or *ExSyn* 292-305. If adjectival position is asked, you will need to consult *Basics* 135-39 or *ExSyn* 306-314. For the usage, you will need to specify whether it is functioning adverbially or substantivally or, if it is functioning as an adjective, specify exactly which form (positive, comparative, superlative) is being used for what sense. For the position, you will need to specify whether the adjective is attributive or predicate and *which* attributive or predicate position it is in.

Warm-Up Passages

Vocabulary

1. πρωΐ : early, early in the morning (Mk 16:9)	7. κατεργάζομαι : I do, accomplish (Ro 2:9)
2. φαίνω : I shine, give light; appear (pass.) (Mk 16:9)	8. ὁ Ἕλλην : a Greek; gentile (Ro 2:9)
3. ἡ Μαρία : Mary (Mk 16:9)	9. παράγω : I go away, pass by (Jn 9:1)
4. ἡ Μαγδαληνή : Magdalene (Mk 16:9)	10. ἡ γενετή : birth (Jn 9:1)
5. ἡ θλῖψις : oppression, affliction; trouble (Ro 2:9)	11. λογίζομαι : I calculate, count, credit, consider, think, evaluate (Ro 4:8)
6. ἡ στενοχωρία : distress, difficulty, anguish (Ro 2:9)	

Mark 16:9

(This is the first verse of the "longer ending" of Mark's Gospel [Mark 16:9-20]. These twelve verses are considered inauthentic by most NT scholars. Our purpose in including Mark 16:9 is not to affirm authenticity, but to serve as an illustration of adjectival usage.)

Ἀναστὰς δὲ πρωΐ πρώτῃ σαββάτου ἐφάνη πρῶτον Μαρίᾳ τῇ Μαγδαληνῇ, παρ' ἧς ἐκβεβλήκει ἑπτὰ δαιμόνια.

1. **πρώτῃ**: Adjectival usage, word related to? (See BDAG, s.v. πρῶτος 1.a.a. for help) [2+1]

_____

• **ἐφάνη** (The subject of this verb is Jesus.)

2. πρῶτον: Adjectival usage, word related to? [2+2]

_____

3. ἑπτά: Adjectival position, word related to? [2+1]

_____

Romans 2:9

θλῖψις καὶ στενοχωρία ἐπὶ πᾶσαν ψυχὴν ἀνθρώπου τοῦ κατεργαζομένου τὸ κακόν, Ἰουδαίου τε πρῶτον καὶ Ἕλληνος.

4. **κατεργαζομένου**: Adjectival position, word related to? (Even though this is a participle, for the purposes of this question treat it as an adjective.) [3+1]

_____

5. **κακόν**: Adjectival usage, word related to? [2+2]

_____

6. **πρῶτον**: Adjectival usage? (This adjective is acting adverbially in the sense that tribulation and anguish will come first to the Jew then to the Greek. What is the other adjectival usage other than adverbial? [See *Basics* 131-35; *ExSyn* 296-305].) [3]

_____

_____

John 9:1

Καὶ παράγων εἶδεν ἄνθρωπον τυφλὸν ἐκ γενετῆς.

7. **τυφλόν**: Adjectival position, word related to? [2+1]

_____

Romans 4:8

μακάριος ἀνὴρ οὗ οὐ μὴ λογίσηται κύριος ἁμαρτίαν.

8. μακάριος: Adjectival position, word related to? [2+1]

Syntax Passages

Matthew 5:17-20

Background

After a brief exposition about the members of the kingdom, Jesus gives several truths about the nature of the kingdom itself (Matt 5:17-7:12). These focus on character development, with a strong emphasis on internal righteousness in an externally ugly world. This is the major section of the Sermon on the Mount, and it is no accident that Jesus begins by linking his views with those of the OT prophets—that is, by giving an exposition of the *intent* of the OT law (5:17-48). Arguably the core of the entire Sermon on the Mount is at the front end of this exposition, for Jesus affirms that the principles of the OT law are inviolable (5:17-20).

Text

5:17 Μὴ νομίσητε ὅτι ἦλθον καταλῦσαι τὸν νόμον ἢ τοὺς προφήτας· οὐκ ἦλθον καταλῦσαι ἀλλὰ πληρῶσαι. **5:18** ἀμὴν γὰρ λέγω ὑμῖν· ἕως ἂν παρέλθη ὁ οὐρανὸς καὶ ἡ γῆ, ἰῶτα ἓν ἢ μία κεραία οὐ μὴ παρέλθη ἀπὸ τοῦ νόμου, ἕως ἂν πάντα γένηται. **5:19** ὃς ἐὰν οὖν λύση μίαν τῶν ἐντολῶν τούτων τῶν ἐλαχίστων καὶ διδάξη οὕτως τοὺς ἀνθρώπους, ἐλάχιστος κληθήσεται ἐν τῇ βασιλείᾳ τῶν οὐρανῶν· ὃς δ᾽ ἂν ποιήση καὶ διδάξη, οὗτος μέγας κληθήσεται ἐν τῇ βασιλείᾳ τῶν οὐρανῶν.

5:20 Λέγω γὰρ ὑμῖν ὅτι ἐὰν μὴ περισσεύση ὑμῶν ἡ δικαιοσύνη πλεῖον τῶν γραμματέων καὶ Φαρισαίων, οὐ μὴ εἰσέλθητε εἰς τὴν βασιλείαν τῶν οὐρανῶν.

Vocabulary

1. νομίζω : I think, believe, hold (v. 17)	5. ἡ κεραία : projection, hook, serif (part of a letter) (v. 18)
2. καταλύω : I detach, destroy; put an end to, abolish (v. 17)	6. λύω : I loose, untie, set free, destroy, abolish, allow (v. 19)
3. παρέρχομαι : I go or pass by; pass away (v. 18)	7. ἐλάχιστος : least, smallest, unimportant (v. 19)
4. τὸ ἰῶτα : iota (v. 18)	8. περισσεύω : I abound, surpass (v. 20)

Matthew 5:17

- **νομίσητε** (This is a prohibitive subjunctive. It is a negative command and is used "to forbid the occurrence of an action" [cf. *Basics* 204–5; *ExSyn* 469]. It can be rendered "do not think.")

- **καταλῦσαι** (This is a purpose infinitive related to ἦλθον. It can be rendered "[I came] in order to destroy …" [cf. *Basics* 256–57; *ExSyn* 590–92].)

Matthew 5:18

9. **ἕν**: Adjectival position, word related to? [2+1]

_____

10. **μία**: Adjective position, word related to? [2+1]

_____

- **οὐ μὴ παρέλθη** (This is an example of an emphatic negation subjunctive. "Emphatic negation is indicated by οὐ μή plus the aorist subjunctive or, less frequently, οὐ μή plus the future indicative (e.g., Matt 26:35; Mark 13:31; John 4:14; 6:35). This is the strongest way to negate something in Greek" [*ExSyn* 468; cf. *Basics* 204; *ExSyn* 468–69].)

11. **πάντα**: Adjectival usage, word related to? [2+1]

_____

Matthew 5:19

12. **ἐλάχιστος**: Adjectival usage? [3]

_____

13. **μέγας**: Adjectival position, word related to? [1+1]

_____

_____

● Matthew 5:20

14. πλεῖον: Adjectival usage, word related to? [3+1]

_____

15. Φαρισαίων: Case, case usage, word related to? [1+1]

_____

Matthew 12:32–36

Background

Within the narrative concerning rising opposition to Jesus and his message (12:1–45), the religious leaders attack the source of Jesus' supernatural power (12:22–37). Immediately after Jesus' strong rebuke of the Pharisees for thinking that he was empowered by the devil (12:25–37, especially 31–32), they ironically ask for more proof of what his spiritual source was (12:38).

● Text

12:32 καὶ ὃς ἐὰν εἴπῃ λόγον κατὰ τοῦ υἱοῦ τοῦ ἀνθρώπου, ἀφεθήσεται αὐτῷ· ὃς δ' ἂν εἴπῃ κατὰ τοῦ πνεύματος τοῦ ἁγίου, οὐκ ἀφεθήσεται αὐτῷ οὔτε ἐν τούτῳ τῷ αἰῶνι οὔτε ἐν τῷ μέλλοντι. **12:33** Ἢ ποιήσατε τὸ δένδρον καλὸν καὶ τὸν καρπὸν αὐτοῦ καλόν, ἢ ποιήσατε τὸ δένδρον σαπρὸν καὶ τὸν καρπὸν αὐτοῦ σαπρόν· ἐκ γὰρ τοῦ καρποῦ τὸ δένδρον γινώσκεται. **12:34** γεννήματα ἐχιδνῶν, πῶς δύνασθε ἀγαθὰ λαλεῖν πονηροὶ ὄντες; ἐκ γὰρ τοῦ περισσεύματος τῆς καρδίας τὸ στόμα λαλεῖ. **12:35** ὁ ἀγαθὸς ἄνθρωπος ἐκ τοῦ ἀγαθοῦ θησαυροῦ ἐκβάλλει ἀγαθά, καὶ ὁ πονηρὸς ἄνθρωπος ἐκ τοῦ πονηροῦ θησαυροῦ ἐκβάλλει πονηρά. **12:36** λέγω δὲ ὑμῖν ὅτι πᾶν ῥῆμα ἀργὸν ὃ λαλήσουσιν οἱ ἄνθρωποι ἀποδώσουσιν περὶ αὐτοῦ λόγον ἐν ἡμέρᾳ κρίσεως.

Vocabulary

1. τὸ δένδρον : tree (v. 33)	6. ὁ θησαυρός : repository, treasure chest, storehouse v. 35)
2. σαπρός : bad, not good; evil (v. 33)	7. ἀργός : unemployed, idle; lazy (v. 36)
3. τὸ γέννημα : child, offspring (v. 34)	8. ἀποδίδωμι : I give up, yield; pay; give account (with λόγος) (v. 36)
4. ἡ ἔχιδνα : snake, viper (v. 34)	9. ἡ κρίσις : judgment, condemnation (v. 36)
5. τὸ περίσσευμα : abundance, fullness; what remains (v. 34)	

Matthew 12:32

16. ἁγίου: Adjectival position, word related to? [2+1]

_____

Matthew 12:33

17. καλόν[1]: Adjectival position, word related to? [2+1]

_____

18. ἤ[2]: What type of conjunction is this? (Give the specific usage listed in *Basics* 293-302 or *ExSyn* 666-78.) [5]

_____

_____

19. σαπρόν[1]: Adjectival position, word related to? [1+1]

_____

Matthew 12:34

20. γεννήματα: Case, case usage, word related to? [1+1+1]

_____

21. ἀγαθά: Adjectival usage, word related to? [2+1]

_____

22. πονηροί: Adjectival position, word related to? [1+2]

_____

- ὄντες (This is a causal participle related δύνασθε ... λαλεῖν. It can be rendered, "[you are unable to speak] ... because you are ..." [cf. *Basics* 275-76; *ExSyn* 631-32].)

Matthew 12:35

23. ἀγαθός[1]: Adjectival position, word related to? [1+1]

_____

24. πονηροῦ: Adjectival position, word related to? [1+1]

_____

25. πονηρά: Adjectival usage, word related to? [2+1]

_____

Matthew 12:36

26. ἀργόν: Adjectival position, word related to? [2+1]

_____

- κρίσεως (This genitive is related to ἡμέρᾳ: "day of judgment." What the exact relationship is, however, is perhaps difficult to determine. The idea seems to be "the day in which mankind will be judged." Perhaps it can be expanded as "the day of their judgment" [possessive genitive?], "the day on which judgment takes place," or simply "the day described by judgment" [descriptive genitive]. For such reasons, it is best simply to classify this as a descriptive genitive [for discussion, see *ExSyn* 81, n. 26].)

Titus 3:8-10

Background

The last part of the body of this letter deals with doing good deeds as a witness to the believers' pagan neighbors in Crete (3:1-14). They should respect the authorities (3:1-2)—especially because the grace of God has changed the condition of their hearts from disobedience to obedience (3:3-4). The author then takes the opportunity of this theme to remind his audience of their own regeneration experience, couching it in almost typically Pauline kerygmatic terms (3:5-7). Part of the way in which the Cretan believers could show that God had done something in their hearts was to major on the majors and avoid silly controversies (3:9-11).

Text

3:8 Πιστὸς ὁ λόγος· καὶ περὶ τούτων βούλομαί σε διαβεβαιοῦσθαι, ἵνα φροντίζωσιν καλῶν ἔργων προΐστασθαι οἱ πεπιστευκότες θεῷ· ταῦτά ἐστιν καλὰ καὶ ὠφέλιμα τοῖς ἀνθρώποις. **3:9** μωρὰς δὲ ζητήσεις καὶ γενεαλογίας καὶ ἔρεις καὶ μάχας νομικὰς περιΐστασο· εἰσὶν γὰρ ἀνωφελεῖς καὶ μάταιοι. **3:10** αἱρετικὸν ἄνθρωπον μετὰ μίαν καὶ δευτέραν νουθεσίαν παραιτοῦ.

Vocabulary

1. βούλομαι : I wish, want, desire (v. 8)	10. ἡ μάχη : battle; fighting, quarrels (pl. in NT) (v. 9)
2. διαβεβαιόομαι : I speak confidently, insist (v. 8)	11. νομικός : about law; legal expert, lawyer (subst.) (v. 9)
3. φροντίζω : I think of, be intent on (v. 8)	12. περιΐστημι : I stand around; avoid, shun (mid.) (v. 9)
4. προΐστημι : I rule, direct; show concern for, engage in, practice (v. 8)	13. ἀνωφελής : useless, harmful (v. 9)
5. ὠφέλιμος : useful, beneficial (v. 8)	14. μάταιος : empty, idle, fruitless (v. 9)
6. μωρός : foolish, stupid (v. 9)	15. αἱρετικός : factious, causing divisions (v. 10)
7. ἡ ζήτησις : investigation; controversial question, controversy (v. 9)	16. δεύτερος : second (v. 10)
8. ἡ γενεαλογία : genealogy (v. 9)	17. ἡ νουθεσία : admonish, instruction, warning (v. 10)
9. ἡ ἔρις : strife, discord; quarrels (pl. in NT) (v. 9)	18. παραιτέομαι : I ask for, beg; reject, avoid (v. 10)

Titus 3:8

27. Πιστός: Adjectival position, word related to? [1+1]

- **ἵνα** (This is a purpose ἵνα clause related to βούλομαι … διαβεβαιοῦσθαι. It can be rendered, "[I want to insist …] so that …" [cf. *Basics* 206; *ExSyn* 472].)

28. καλῶν: Adjectival position, word related to? [2+1]

- προΐστασθαι (This is a complementary infinitive related to φροντίζωσιν. Complementary infinitives are "very frequently used with 'helper' verbs to complete their thought" [*ExSyn* 598; cf. *Basics* 259; *ExSyn* 598-99]. It can be rendered, "[so that the ones who placed their faith in God might be careful] to practice.")

- οἱ πεπιστευκότες (This is a substantival participle acting as the subject of φροντίζωσιν even though it is separated by several words [cf. *Basics* 270-71; *ExSyn* 619-21].)

29. ὠφέλιμα: Adjectival position, word related to? [2+1]

Titus 3:9

30. μωράς: Adjectival position, word related to? [2+2]

- ἔρεις (Several important MSS have the singular reading ἔριν instead [ℵ* Dᵍʳ* F G 999 arm eth *al.*]. Most MSS, though, have the plural reading ἔρεις, which appears in our text [A C K L P 075 0142 and many others]. The UBS text has the plural reading. However, the singular reading cannot easily be explained if the plural was the original; scribes would be tempted to change the singular to the plural so that it would agree with the other plurals in the context, but not vice versa. For this reason the singular reading seems to be preferable.)

31. νομικάς: Adjectival position, word related to? [2+1]

- περιΐστασο (Notice that the author of this letter, at times, places the verb at the end of the clause [cf. 3:10].)

32. ἀνωφελεῖς: Adjectival usage, word related to? [2+1]

Titus 3:10

33. αἱρετικόν: Adjectival usage, word related to? [2+1]

Lesson 8: Person and Number; Active Voice

Warm-Up Passages

Vocabulary

1. μεταμορφόω : I transfigure, change (pass. in NT) (Mt 17:2)	7. συλλαλέω : I talk, discuss (Mt 17:3)
2. ἔμπροσθεν : in front of, ahead (Mt 17:2)	8. διατρίβω : I spend time, stay, remain (Jn 3:22)
3. λάμπω : I shine, flash, gleam (Mt 17:2)	9. καίτοιγε : although (Jn 4:2)
4. ὁ ἥλιος : sun (Mt 17:2)	10. ἡ Ἀσία : Asia (1 Co 16:19)
5. λευκός : bright, shining; white (Mt 17:2)	11. ὁ Ἀκύλας : Aquila (1 Co 16:19)
6. ὁ Ἠλίας : Elijah (Mt 17:3)	12. ἡ Πρίσκα : Prisca (1 Co 16:19)

Matthew 17:2–3

17:2 καὶ μετεμορφώθη ἔμπροσθεν αὐτῶν, καὶ ἔλαμψεν τὸ πρόσωπον αὐτοῦ ὡς ὁ ἥλιος, τὰ δὲ ἱμάτια αὐτοῦ ἐγένετο λευκὰ ὡς τὸ φῶς. **17:3** καὶ ἰδοὺ ὤφθη αὐτοῖς Μωϋσῆς καὶ Ἠλίας συλλαλοῦντες μετ' αὐτοῦ.

- **μετεμορφώθη** (The subject of this verb is Jesus [see 17:1].)

1. **ἐγένετο**: Why is this verb singular (state the specific rule)? What word is it related to? [2+2]

_____

_____

2. **ὤφθη**: What is the subject of this verb? State the rule that this construction follows, and indicate its significance here. [3+3+3]

_____

_____

● John 3:22

Μετὰ ταῦτα ἦλθεν ὁ Ἰησοῦς καὶ οἱ μαθηταὶ αὐτοῦ εἰς τὴν Ἰουδαίαν γῆν καὶ ἐκεῖ διέτριβεν μετ᾽ αὐτῶν καὶ ἐβάπτιζεν.

3. **ἦλθεν**: What is the subject of this verb? State the rule that this construction follows, and indicate its significance here. [2+2+2]

_____

_____

4. **ἐβάπτιζεν**: Voice, voice usage? [2+3]

_____

_____

John 4:1–2

● **4:1** Ὡς οὖν ἔγνω ὁ Ἰησοῦς ὅτι ἤκουσαν οἱ Φαρισαῖοι ὅτι Ἰησοῦς πλείονας μαθητὰς ποιεῖ καὶ βαπτίζει ἢ Ἰωάννης **4:2**—καίτοιγε Ἰησοῦς αὐτὸς οὐκ ἐβάπτιζεν ἀλλ᾽ οἱ μαθηταὶ αὐτοῦ.

5. **Ὡς**: Scan the entry in BDAG on ὡς. What usage fits best here? [4]

_____

_____

- **οὖν** (This word basically functions as an inferential conjunction or a transitional conjunction. In John's Gospel especially it is used simply to mark a transition in the narrative, rather than a logical consequence or inference from the preceding. "Then" is an appropriate gloss.)

- **ὅτι** (Both instances of ὅτι in this verse introduce indirect discourse. John 4:1 involves an indirect discourse *within* an indirect discourse. In such instances, the translation should be removed by one time-frame because of English usage. That is, instead of translating ἤκουσαν as "heard," it should be translated as "had heard"; instead of translating ποιεῖ as "is making," it should be translated as "was making." For more help on indirect discourse, see *Basics* 198–99; *ExSyn* 456-58.)

● 6. **βαπτίζει**: Voice, voice usage? [1+2]

_____

7. μαθηταί: Case, case usage, word related to (give exact Greek form)? [1+1+2]

_____

1 Corinthians 16:19

Ἀσπάζονται ὑμᾶς αἱ ἐκκλησίαι τῆς Ἀσίας. ἀσπάζεται ὑμᾶς ἐν κυρίῳ πολλὰ Ἀκύλας καὶ Πρίσκα σὺν τῇ κατ᾽ οἶκον αὐτῶν ἐκκλησίᾳ.

8. ἀσπάζεται: What is the subject of this verb? State the rule that this construction follows and indicate its significance here. [3+2+3]

_____

_____

- ἀσπάζεται (The plural form of this verb, ἀσπάζονται, is found in several good MSS [B F G 075 0121 0243 33 1739 1881] as well as the Byzantine minuscules. But the singular is read by an equally impressive group [ℵ C D K P Ψ 104 2464 *pc*]. The singular appears to have given rise to the plural: [1] The rest of the greetings in this verse are in the plural; this one was probably made plural by some scribes for purposes of assimilation; and, more significantly, [2] since both Aquila and Prisca are mentioned as the ones who send the greeting, the plural is more natural.)

Syntax Passages

Philippians 2:6-11

Background

The apostle exhorts his readers to live humbly as servants of Christ (2:1-11). He appeals to them on the basis of membership in the body of Christ (2:1-4), reminding them that selfishness hurts everyone. Then he seems to weave an early Christian hymn into the fabric of his argument. The *kenosis* (or "emptying") (2:6-11) functions as a reminder for them to follow in the steps of Christ: if he who was in the "form of God" could humble himself, what right do believers have to refrain from doing the same thing? After Christ "emptied himself" (by adding humanity, 2:6-8) God exalted him (2:9-11).

Text

2:6 ὃς ἐν μορφῇ θεοῦ ὑπάρχων
οὐχ ἁρπαγμὸν ἡγήσατο
τὸ εἶναι ἴσα θεῷ,

2:7 ἀλλὰ ἑαυτὸν ἐκένωσεν
μορφὴν δούλου λαβών,
ἐν ὁμοιώματι ἀνθρώπων γενόμενος·
καὶ σχήματι εὑρεθεὶς ὡς ἄνθρωπος
2:8 ἐταπείνωσεν ἑαυτὸν
γενόμενος ὑπήκοος μέχρι θανάτου,
θανάτου δὲ σταυροῦ.
2:9 διὸ καὶ ὁ θεὸς αὐτὸν ὑπερύψωσεν
καὶ ἐχαρίσατο αὐτῷ τὸ ὄνομα
τὸ ὑπὲρ πᾶν ὄνομα,
2:10 ἵνα ἐν τῷ ὀνόματι Ἰησοῦ
πᾶν γόνυ κάμψῃ
ἐπουρανίων καὶ ἐπιγείων καὶ καταχθονίων
2:11 καὶ πᾶσα γλῶσσα ἐξομολογήσηται ὅτι
κύριος Ἰησοῦς Χριστὸς
εἰς δόξαν θεοῦ πατρός.

Vocabulary

1. ἡ μορφή : form; outward appearance (v. 6)	11. ὁ σταυρός : cross (lit. and fig.) (v. 8)
2. ὁ ἁρπαγμός : something to grasp; prize (v. 6)	12. ὑπερυψόω : I raise, exalt (v. 9)
3. ἡγέομαι : I think, consider, regard (v. 6)	13. χαρίζομαι : I give graciously, grant; forgive, pardon (v. 9)
4. ἴσος : equal, same, consistent (v. 6)	14. τὸ γόνυ : knee (v. 10)
5. κενόω : I empty, divest of prestige (v. 7)	15. κάμπτω : I bend, bow (v. 10)
6. τὸ ὁμοίωμα : likeness; image, appearance (v. 7)	16. ἐπουράνιος : heavenly; heavenly things (subst.); in heaven (v. 10)
7. τὸ σχῆμα : outward appearance, form; way of life (v. 7)	17. ἐπίγειος : earthly, on earth; worldly things (subst.) (v. 10)
8. ταπεινόω : I lower; humble (v. 8)	18. καταχθόνιος : under the earth, subterranean; a being under the earth (subst.) (v. 10)
9. ὑπήκοος : obedient (v. 8)	19. ἐξομολογέω : I promise; confess (mid.); acknowledge (v. 11)
10. μέχρι : until; as far as (v. 8)	

Philippians 2:6

- **τὸ εἶναι ἴσα θεῷ** (This infinitive clause acts as the object of the verb ἡγήσατο in an object-complement construction. It can be rendered "equality with God.")

- **τό** (Some have argued that this article is anaphoric referring back to μορφῇ θεοῦ.* It is more likely that the article is simply distinguishing the object from the complement ἁρπαγμόν in this object-complement construction [cf. *Basics* 108; *ExSyn* 242-43].)

9. **ὑπάρχων**: Voice, voice usage? [2+2]

___

Philippians 2:7

10. **ἐκένωσεν**: Voice, voice usage? [2+3]

___

Philippians 2:8

11. **ἐταπείνωσεν**: Voice, voice usage? [2+2]

___

- **δέ** (BDF tell us that this conjunction can be used as "an explanation or an intensification." They give the gloss "but," or "and … at that" [BDF §448(8)].)

- **σταυροῦ** (This may be a genitive of production, a genitive of place, or a genitive of means. Jesus' death was brought about or produced by the cross [production], took place on the cross [place], or came about by means of the cross [means] [cf. *ExSyn* 104-6].)

Philippians 2:9

- **καί¹** (This is a connective conjunction; here it is being used adjunctively and can be translated "also" [cf. *Basics* 296; *ExSyn* 671].)

___

* N. T. Wright, "ἁρπαγμός and the Meaning of Philippians 2:5-11," *JTS*, NS 37 (1986): 344. But see now Denny Burk, "On the Articular Infinitive in Philippians 2:6: A Grammatical Note with Christological Implications," *TynBul* 55 (2004): 253-74.

12. τό²: Treat this article as a function marker. What is its specific use? [3]

Philippians 2:10

- **ἵνα** (This is a ἵνα of purpose-result related to ἐχαρίσατο. This category normally occurs when God is the subject. The idea is that God accomplishes what he purposes. It can be rendered, "[and granted to him the name] … so that …" [cf. *Basics* 206-7; *ExSyn* 473-74].)

13. κάμψῃ: Voice, voice usage? [2+2]

- **ἐπουρανίων καὶ ἐπιγείων καὶ καταχθονίων** (These three adjectives are acting as substantives and are functioning as either genitives of place or possession. If place, then they are modifying the verb κάμψῃ and indicating the place where this action occurred, "every knee should bow, in the heavenly and earthly and subterranean places." They could also be functioning as possessive genitives modifying γόνυ, "the knees of those in heaven, etc." [*ExSyn* 125 n. 142].)

Colossians 1:9, 13–20

Background

The first major section of Colossians, on the positive presentation of the sufficiency of Christ, involves four parts, two of which are seen in the lesson here: (1) thanksgiving for the Colossians because of their positive response to the gospel (1:3-8), coupled with a prayer for them to grow in knowledge and productivity (1:9-14). This prayer deals, though very subtly, with the heart of the epistle: the heretics claim to have a superior knowledge, yet their very philosophy chokes out any productivity for God (cf. 2:20-23). (2) Without so much as an "Amen" to the prayer, the author continues with a recital of an early Christian hymn in which Christ is magnified as Deity in the flesh, as the Creator incarnate (1:15-20).

Text

1:9 Διὰ τοῦτο καὶ ἡμεῖς, ἀφ᾽ ἧς ἡμέρας ἠκούσαμεν, οὐ παυόμεθα ὑπὲρ ὑμῶν προσευχόμενοι καὶ αἰτούμενοι, ἵνα πληρωθῆτε τὴν ἐπίγνωσιν τοῦ θελήματος αὐτοῦ ἐν πάσῃ σοφίᾳ καὶ συνέσει πνευματικῇ, … **1:13** ὃς ἐρρύσατο ἡμᾶς ἐκ τῆς ἐξουσίας τοῦ σκότους καὶ μετέστησεν εἰς τὴν βασιλείαν τοῦ υἱοῦ τῆς ἀγάπης αὐτοῦ, **1:14** ἐν ᾧ ἔχομεν τὴν ἀπολύτρωσιν, τὴν ἄφεσιν τῶν ἁμαρτιῶν·

1:15 ὅς ἐστιν εἰκὼν τοῦ θεοῦ τοῦ ἀοράτου,
πρωτότοκος πάσης κτίσεως,
1:16 ὅτι ἐν αὐτῷ ἐκτίσθη τὰ πάντα
ἐν τοῖς οὐρανοῖς καὶ ἐπὶ τῆς γῆς,
τὰ ὁρατὰ καὶ τὰ ἀόρατα,
εἴτε θρόνοι εἴτε κυριότητες
εἴτε ἀρχαὶ εἴτε ἐξουσίαι·
τὰ πάντα δι᾽ αὐτοῦ καὶ εἰς αὐτὸν ἔκτισται·
1:17 καὶ αὐτός ἐστιν πρὸ πάντων
καὶ τὰ πάντα ἐν αὐτῷ συνέστηκεν,
1:18 καὶ αὐτός ἐστιν ἡ κεφαλὴ τοῦ σώματος τῆς ἐκκλησίας·
ὅς ἐστιν ἀρχή,
πρωτότοκος ἐκ τῶν νεκρῶν,
ἵνα γένηται ἐν πᾶσιν αὐτὸς πρωτεύων,
1:19 ὅτι ἐν αὐτῷ εὐδόκησεν πᾶν τὸ πλήρωμα κατοικῆσαι
1:20 καὶ δι᾽ αὐτοῦ ἀποκαταλλάξαι τὰ πάντα εἰς αὐτόν,
εἰρηνοποιήσας διὰ τοῦ αἵματος τοῦ σταυροῦ αὐτοῦ,
δι᾽ αὐτοῦ εἴτε τὰ ἐπὶ τῆς γῆς
εἴτε τὰ ἐν τοῖς οὐρανοῖς.

Vocabulary

1. παύω : I stop, hinder; cease (v. 9)	14. κτίζω : to create, make (v. 16)
2. ἡ ἐπίγνωσις : knowledge, consciousness (v. 9)	15. ὁρατός : visible (v. 16)
3. ἡ σύνεσις : intelligence, acuteness; insight (v. 9)	16. ἡ κυριότης : lordship; angelic powers, dominions (v. 16)
4. πνευματικός : caused by or filled with the (divine) spirit, spiritual (v. 9)	17. πρό : before (v. 17)
5. ῥύομαι : I save, rescue, deliver (v. 13)	18. συνίστημι : I exist, hold together; present; show (v. 17)
6. τὸ σκότος : darkness (v. 13)	19. πρωτεύω : I am first, have first place (v. 18)
7. μεθίστημι : I remove, transfer; turn away (v. 13)	20. εὐδοκέω : I consent, determine; I am well pleased (v. 19)
8. ἡ ἀπολύτρωσις : release; redemption (v. 14)	21. τὸ πλήρωμα : that which fills (up); full measure (v. 19)
9. ἡ ἄφεσις : release; pardon; forgiveness (v. 14)	22. κατοικέω : I live, dwell, reside (v. 19)
10. ἡ εἰκών : likeness, portrait; appearance; image (v. 15)	23. ἀποκαταλλάσσω : I reconcile (v. 20)

11. ἀόρατος : unseen, invisible (v. 15)	24. εἰρηνοποιέω : I make peace (v. 20)
12. πρωτότοκος : firstborn (lit.); firstborn (fig. of Christ and God's people) (v. 15)	25. ὁ σταυρός : cross (fig. and lit.) (v. 20)
13. ἡ κτίσις : creation, world (v. 15)	

Colossians 1:9

- ἀφ' ἧς (This phrase has become "a fixed formula" that "indicates the point from which someth. begins" [BDAG s.v. ἀπό 2β]. The noun that follows usually indicates the temporal point; in this case it is "the day we heard.")

14. ἠκούσαμεν: Use of first person? [4]

- ἠκούσαμεν (There is no direct object stated with this verb that describes the content of what was "heard." This leaves this passage somewhat ambiguous. It probably refers to the Colossians' spirituality, which is the focus of the previous paragraph [vv. 3-8]. For this reason most English translations add an object to clarify the sense of the verse. The translations vary between "it" [so KJV, NASB, NRSV] or "about you" [NET, TEV, NIV, NLT].)

15. παυόμεθα: Use of person? [3]

- προσευχόμενοι καὶ αἰτούμενοι (These are complementary participles that "complete the thought of another verb." Here they complete the thought of παυόμεθα and can be rendered "[we have not ceased ...] praying and asking" [ExSyn 646].)

Colossians 1:13

16. ἡμᾶς: Use of person? [4]

Colossians 1:14

17. ἔχομεν: Person, person usage? [1+2]

- τὴν ἀπολύτρωσιν (Several minor MSS have the reading διὰ τοῦ αἵματος αὐτοῦ. As Metzger points out, this is most likely an interpolation from Eph 1:7 [Metzger, *Textual Commentary*[2], 554]. The preferred reading also has strong external support [ℵ A C D F G 1739].)

Colossians 1:15

18. ἐστιν: Voice, voice usage? [1+1]

_____

Colossians 1:16

- ὅτι (This is a causal conjunction and could be rendered "for" or "because" [cf. *Basics* 200-201; *ExSyn* 460-61].)

19. ἐκτίσθη: Why is this verb singular (state the specific rule)? What word is it related to? [3+2]

_____

Colossians 1:17

20. συνέστηκεν: Look this word up in BDAG and find the reference to this verse. Based on the lexical meaning that BDAG assigns to συνίστημι here, what is the most likely usage of its voice? [2]

_____

Colossians 1:18

- ἵνα (This is a ἵνα of purpose-result related to ἐστιν[2]. This category normally occurs when God is the subject. The idea is that God accomplished what he purposed. It can be rendered, "[who is the beginning] ... so that ..." [cf. *Basics* 206-7; *ExSyn* 473-74].)

- πρωτεύων (See BDAG on this participle. It may be taken adjectivally in the predicate, or substantivally. The reason for the participle rather than πρῶτος is most likely due to metric considerations in the hymn of Col 1:15-20.)

Colossians 1:19

- ὅτι (This is a causal conjunction and can be rendered "for" or "because" [cf. *Basics* 200-201; *ExSyn* 460-61].)

21. εὐδόκησεν: Voice, voice usage? [1+2]

_____

22. κατοικῆσαι: Voice, voice usage? (This is a complementary infinitive related to εὐδόκησεν [cf. *Basics* 259-60; *ExSyn* 598-99].) [1+2]

_____

Colossians 1:20

23. ἀποκαταλλάξαι: Voice, voice usage? (This is a complementary infinitive related to εὐδόκησεν [cf. *Basics* 259-60; *ExSyn* 598-99].) [2+2]

_____

24. εἰρηνοποιήσας: Voice, voice usage? (This is an instrumental participle related to ἀποκαταλλάξαι. It can be rendered, "[to reconcile all things unto him] by making peace ..." [cf. *Basics* 274-75; *ExSyn* 628-30].) [2+2]

_____

- δι' αὐτοῦ[2] (Both the exclusion [B D* F G I 0278 81 1175 1739 1881 2464 *al* latt sa] and inclusion [P[46] A C D[1] Ψ 048[vid] 33 *Byz*] of the phrase δι' αὐτοῦ have strong external support. However, "internal evidence points to the inclusion of the phrase as original. The word immediately preceding the phrase is the masculine pronoun αὐτοῦ; thus the possibility of omission through homoioteleuton in various witnesses is likely. Scribes might have deleted the phrase because of perceived redundancy or awkwardness in the sense: The shorter reading is smoother and more elegant, so scribes would be prone to correct the text in that direction. As far as style is concerned, repetition of key words and phrases for emphasis is not foreign to the *corpus Paulinum* (see, e.g., Rom 8:23, Eph 1:13, 2 Cor 12:7). In short, it is easier to account for the shorter reading arising from the longer reading than vice versa, so the longer reading is more likely original" [NET-Nestle, *Text-Critical Notes* 867].)

Lesson 9: Middle and Passive Voice

Warm-Up Passages

Vocabulary

1. προσλαμβάνω : (mid. in NT) to take aside (Mt 16:22)	5. τρίμηνος : (period of) three months (Heb 11:23)
2. ἐπιτιμάω : I rebuke, warn (Mt 16:22)	6. διότι : because, therefore, for (Heb 11:23)
3. ἵλεως : gracious, merciful (Mt 16:22) The idiom ἵλεώς σοι means "God forbid!"	7. ἀστεῖος : handsome, well-bred (Heb 11:23)
4. κρύπτω : I hide, keep secret (Heb 11:23)	8. τὸ διάταγμα : edict, command (Heb 11:23)

Matthew 16:22

καὶ προσλαβόμενος αὐτὸν ὁ Πέτρος ἤρξατο ἐπιτιμᾶν αὐτῷ λέγων· ἵλεώς σοι, κύριε· οὐ μὴ ἔσται σοι τοῦτο.

1. **προσλαβόμενος**: Voice, voice usage? [2+3]

_____

John 17:7

νῦν ἔγνωκαν ὅτι πάντα ὅσα δέδωκάς μοι παρὰ σοῦ εἰσιν.

2. **παρά**: What type of agency is expressed by this preposition? [3]

_____

_____

Hebrews 11:23

Πίστει Μωϋσῆς γεννηθεὶς ἐκρύβη τρίμηνον ὑπὸ τῶν πατέρων αὐτοῦ, διότι εἶδον ἀστεῖον τὸ παιδίον καὶ οὐκ ἐφοβήθησαν τὸ διάταγμα τοῦ βασιλέως.

3. Πίστει: What type of agency is expressed by this noun? [3]

_____

4. ἐκρύβη: In what type of passive construction is this verb? (The passive verb occurs with an accusative word, but this is not the same as a passive with a retained object. The accusative adjective τρίμηνον indicates the extent of time that the baby was hidden. Look for something else in the context that indicates the structural category of the passive verb.) [4]

_____

5. διότι: Classify this conjunction. [3]

_____

Syntax Passages

Philippians 1:15–30

Background

The apostle turns to his own circumstances, which the Philippians have been desperate to learn about (1:12-26). Without so much as giving any details to invoke sympathy, Paul boldly states that his circumstances have advanced the gospel (1:12). He is evidently more concerned about the gospel than about his own life and thus begins to detail the effect that the gospel has had: (1) the praetorian guard has heard the good news (1:13) and many have responded, and (2) other evangelists have been emboldened by Paul's imprisonment (1:14).

But some of these evangelists have gained courage in their preaching for the wrong reasons, viz., to make Paul jealous (1:15, 17), while others are properly courageous (1:15, 16). What is Paul's attitude toward all this? (1) Toward the evangelists, he is pleased that the gospel is being proclaimed regardless of the motive (1:18). (2) Toward Christ, he longs to be with him since Christ is his whole reason for living (1:19-23). (3) Toward the Philippians, because he can still impact their lives, he knows that he will be joined to them again (1:19-26).

By concluding the section on his own circumstances with a note about his continued ministry to the Philippians, Paul now, appropriately enough, continues his ministry to the Philippians! The real heart of the epistle is seen in 1:27-2:30 where Paul instructs the church in matters of sanctification. Paul draws on the political background of Philippi (viz., it is a free city) and encourages the believers to live boldly as citizens of _heaven_ (1:27-30). Such bold living, in the face of opposition, will be a sign to their opponents that God is both with the Christians and against their enemies.

Text

1:15 τινὲς μὲν καὶ διὰ φθόνον καὶ ἔριν, τινὲς δὲ καὶ δι' εὐδοκίαν τὸν Χριστὸν κηρύσσουσιν· **1:16** οἱ μὲν ἐξ ἀγάπης, εἰδότες ὅτι εἰς ἀπολογίαν τοῦ εὐαγγελίου κεῖμαι, **1:17** οἱ δὲ ἐξ ἐριθείας τὸν Χριστὸν καταγγέλλουσιν, οὐχ ἁγνῶς, οἰόμενοι θλῖψιν ἐγείρειν τοῖς δεσμοῖς μου. **1:18** Τί γάρ; πλὴν ὅτι παντὶ τρόπῳ, εἴτε προφάσει εἴτε ἀληθείᾳ, Χριστὸς καταγγέλλεται, καὶ ἐν τούτῳ χαίρω.

Ἀλλὰ καὶ χαρήσομαι, **1:19** οἶδα γὰρ ὅτι τοῦτό μοι ἀποβήσεται εἰς σωτηρίαν διὰ τῆς ὑμῶν δεήσεως καὶ ἐπιχορηγίας τοῦ πνεύματος Ἰησοῦ Χριστοῦ **1:20** κατὰ τὴν ἀποκαραδοκίαν καὶ ἐλπίδα μου, ὅτι ἐν οὐδενὶ αἰσχυνθήσομαι ἀλλ' ἐν πάσῃ παρρησίᾳ ὡς πάντοτε καὶ νῦν μεγαλυνθήσεται Χριστὸς ἐν τῷ σώματί μου, εἴτε διὰ ζωῆς εἴτε διὰ θανάτου. **1:21** Ἐμοὶ γὰρ τὸ ζῆν Χριστὸς καὶ τὸ ἀποθανεῖν κέρδος. **1:22** εἰ δὲ τὸ ζῆν ἐν σαρκί, τοῦτό μοι καρπὸς ἔργου, καὶ τί αἱρήσομαι οὐ γνωρίζω. **1:23** συνέχομαι δὲ ἐκ τῶν δύο, τὴν ἐπιθυμίαν ἔχων εἰς τὸ ἀναλῦσαι καὶ σὺν Χριστῷ εἶναι, πολλῷ γὰρ μᾶλλον κρεῖσσον· **1:24** τὸ δὲ ἐπιμένειν ἐν τῇ σαρκὶ ἀναγκαιότερον δι' ὑμᾶς. **1:25** καὶ τοῦτο πεποιθὼς οἶδα ὅτι μενῶ καὶ παραμενῶ πᾶσιν ὑμῖν εἰς τὴν ὑμῶν προκοπὴν καὶ χαρὰν τῆς πίστεως, **1:26** ἵνα τὸ καύχημα ὑμῶν περισσεύῃ ἐν Χριστῷ Ἰησοῦ ἐν ἐμοὶ διὰ τῆς ἐμῆς παρουσίας πάλιν πρὸς ὑμᾶς.

1:27 Μόνον ἀξίως τοῦ εὐαγγελίου τοῦ Χριστοῦ πολιτεύεσθε, ἵνα εἴτε ἐλθὼν καὶ ἰδὼν ὑμᾶς εἴτε ἀπὼν ἀκούω τὰ περὶ ὑμῶν, ὅτι στήκετε ἐν ἑνὶ πνεύματι, μιᾷ ψυχῇ συναθλοῦντες τῇ πίστει τοῦ εὐαγγελίου **1:28** καὶ μὴ πτυρόμενοι ἐν μηδενὶ ὑπὸ τῶν ἀντικειμένων, ἥτις ἐστὶν αὐτοῖς ἔνδειξις ἀπωλείας, ὑμῶν δὲ σωτηρίας, καὶ τοῦτο ἀπὸ θεοῦ· **1:29** ὅτι ὑμῖν ἐχαρίσθη τὸ ὑπὲρ Χριστοῦ, οὐ μόνον τὸ εἰς αὐτὸν πιστεύειν ἀλλὰ καὶ τὸ ὑπὲρ αὐτοῦ πάσχειν, **1:30** τὸν αὐτὸν ἀγῶνα ἔχοντες, οἷον εἴδετε ἐν ἐμοὶ καὶ νῦν ἀκούετε ἐν ἐμοί.

Vocabulary

1. ὁ φθόνος : envy, jealousy (v. 15)	26. γνωρίζω : I know, make known, reveal (v. 22)
2. ἡ ἔρις : strife, discord, contentions (v. 15)	27. συνέχω : I step, shut; guard; am distressed, hard-presesed (to choose) (v. 23)
3. ἡ εὐδοκία : good will; favor (v. 15)	28. ἡ ἐπιθυμία : desire, longing; craving (v. 23)
4. ἡ ἀπολογία : defense (speech), reply (v. 16)	29. ἀναλύω : I depart, return, die (v. 23)
5. κεῖμαι : I lie, recline; be appointed, set, destined (v. 16)	30. ἐπιμένω : I stay, remain; continue (v. 24)
6. ἡ ἐριθεία : strife, selfishness; disputes (pl.) (v. 17)	31. ἀναγκαῖος : necessary; intimate, close (v. 24)
7. καταγγέλλω : I proclaim, announce (v. 17)	32. παραμένω : I remain, stay; continue (v. 25)
8. ἁγνῶς : purely, sincerely (v. 17)	33. ἡ προκοπή : progress, advancement (v. 25)
9. οἴομαι : I think, suppose, expect (v. 17)	34. τὸ καύχημα : boast, object of boasting (v. 26)
10. ἡ θλῖψις : oppression, affliction (v. 17)	35. περισσεύω : I abound, surpass; excel (v. 26)
11. ὁ δεσμός : bond, fetter; prison, imprisonment (pl.) (v. 17)	36. ἡ παρουσία : presence; coming, advent (v. 26)

12. πλήν : but, nevertheless; except (v. 18)	37. ἀξίως : worthily (v. 27)
13. ὁ τρόπος : manner, way; kind of life (v. 18)	38. πολιτεύομαι : I live, lead my life (v. 27)
14. ἡ πρόφασις : actual motive or reason; excuse; pretext, for appearance sake (v. 18)	39. ἄπειμι : I am absent, away (v. 27)
15. ἀποβαίνω : I go away, get out; turn out (v. 19)	40. στήκω : I stand; be steadfast (v. 27)
16. ἡ σωτηρία : deliverance; salvation (v. 19)	41. συναθλέω : I contend or struggle along with (v. 27)
17. ἡ δέησις : prayer (v. 19)	42. πτύρω : I am terrified, intimidated (v. 28)
18. ἡ ἐπιχορηγία : assistance, support (v. 19)	43. ἀντίκειμαι I am opposed to; opponent (subst. ptc.) (v. 28)
19. ἡ ἀποκαραδοκία : eager expectation (v. 20)	44. ἡ ἔνδειξις : sign; proof, demonstration (v. 28)
20. αἰσχύνω : I am ashamed; put to shame (mid. and pass. in NT) (v. 20)	45. ἡ ἀπώλεια : waste, ruin (v. 28)
21. ἡ παρρησία : outspokenness, frankness; confidence, boldness (v. 20)	46. χαρίζομαι : give; cancel; forgive (v. 29)
22. πάντοτε : always, at all times (v. 20)	47. πάσχω : I experience; suffer, endure (v. 29)
23. μεγαλύνω : make great; exalt; be glorified (v. 20)	48. ὁ ἀγών : contest, race; struggle, fight (fig. in NT) (v. 30)
24. τὸ κέρδος : gain, profit (v. 21)	49. οἷος : of what sort, (such) as (v. 30)
25. αἱρέω : I choose, prefer (mid. in NT) (v. 22)	

Philippians 1:17

- οἱ (This article is acting as a personal pronoun and refers back to the ones [τινές] preaching Christ from envy [φθόνον] and rivalry [ἔριν] in 1:15 [cf. *Basics* 95; *ExSyn* 211–12]. Recall that the article can only function this way when it is nominative and is followed by μέν or δέ.)

- Verses 15–17 ([15] τινὲς μὲν καὶ διὰ φθόνον καὶ ἔριν, τινὲς δὲ καὶ δι᾽ εὐδοκίαν τὸν Χριστὸν κηρύσσουσιν· [16] οἱ μὲν ἐξ ἀγάπης … [17] οἱ δὲ ἐξ ἐριθείας …) constitute a *chiasmus* or *chiasm* (sometimes called a reverse parallel). This is a literary device in which two or more elements are mentioned at the beginning of a discourse and are developed in reverse order. In v. 15, the first group named are people preaching Christ for the wrong reasons; this is followed by those who are preaching Christ with proper motives. In v. 16 "these" [οἱ μέν] are the same as the second group in v. 15, while in v. 17 "these" are the same as the first group mentioned in v. 15. The pattern thus is a simple chiasmus involving only two elements, each of which is repeated in reverse order:

A   those who preach with wrong motives

   B   those who preach with right motives

   B' those who preach with right motives

A' those who preach with wrong motives.

Chiasm is a common stylistic idiom in the OT (especially the Psalms), though less common in the NT. Recognizing this pattern may uncover the emphasis of various portions of Scripture, including whole books (e.g., Romans, Galatians, Titus). (See BDF §476[2]).) Elsewhere in the NT, the chiasm is sometimes very developed, involving as many as five or six elements.

6. οἰόμενοι: Voice, voice usage? (This is a participle of cause related to καταγγέλλουσιν [cf. *Basics* 275-76; *ExSyn* 631-32].) [2+2]

___

Philippians 1:18

7. πλήν: Classify the conjunction and give a translation suitable to this context after consulting BDAG. [2+2]

___

8 καταγγέλλεται: Voice, voice usage? [2+2]

___

9. χαρήσομαι: Voice, voice usage? [2+2]

___

Philippians 1:19

10. μοι: Case, case usage, word related to? [1+2+1]

___

• τῆς ὑμῶν δεήσεως καὶ ἐπιχορηγίας (These nouns are in an impersonal TSKS construction [article-substantive-καί-substantive]. The force of such a construction is tied to whether the substantives are singular or plural, personal or impersonal, and proper names or common epithets, and whether they are substantival adjectives, substantival participles, or nouns. All such constructions put an accent on the *unity* of the substantives. Beyond unity, equality or even identity of referents can also be inferred from various patterns within the TSKS construction. The impersonal TSKS construction hardly ever has the force of identical referents, though overlap or even hendiadys [in which one noun functions as an adjective modifying the other noun] does occur. In this instance, it most likely means "your prayer[s] and other support" or, more likely, "your supportive prayers" [thus, hendiadys]. See *Basics* 120-28; *ExSyn* 270-90.)

Philippians 1:20

11. τὴν ἀποκαραδοκίαν καὶ ἐλπίδα μου: What kind of articular construction is this? What is the most likely semantic force? (See *Basics* 120-28; *ExSyn* 270-90 for help.) [2+2]

_____

12. ἐν[1]: Assuming that this preposition expresses agency, what type of agency is expressed? [2]

_____

13. αἰσχυνθήσομαι: Voice, voice usage? [2+2]

_____

14. μεγαλυνθήσεται: Voice, voice usage? [2+2]

_____

Philippians 1:21

15. τὸ ζῆν ... τὸ ἀποθανεῖν: These infinitives are acting as the subjects of implied εἰμί's. They can be rendered, "to live [is Christ] ... to die [is gain]" (cf. *Basics* 260-61; *ExSyn* 600-1). On what basis can we claim that these infinitives are the subjects instead of the predicate nominatives? [3]

_____

Philippians 1:22

16. αἱρήσομαι: Voice, voice usage? [2+2]

_____

Philippians 1:23

17. συνέχομαι: Voice, voice usage? [2+2]

- ἔχων (This is a participle of cause related to συνέχομαι. It can be rendered, "[I am torn] … because I have …" [cf. *Basics* 275-76; *ExSyn* 631-32].)

- εἰς τὸ ἀναλῦσαι … εἶναι (These are epexegetical infinitives related to ἐπιθυμίαν. They can be rendered, "[having the desire], namely, to depart and to be" [cf. *Basics* 263; *ExSyn* 607].)

Philippians 1:24

- τὸ … ἐπιμένειν (This infinitive is acting as the subject of an implied εἰμί. It can be rendered, "to remain [in the flesh is]" [cf. *Basics* 260-61; *ExSyn* 600-1].)

- ἀναγκαιότερον (This is a comparative adjective in predicate relation to τὸ … ἐπιμένειν. It is neuter most likely because of concord with the neuter singular subject.)

Philippians 1:25

- πεποιθώς (This is a participle of cause related to οἶδα. It can be rendered, "because I am confident … [I know]" [cf. *Basics* 275-76; *ExSyn* 631-32].)

Philippians 1:26

- ἵνα (This is a purpose ἵνα related to μενῶ and παραμενῶ [v. 25]. It can be rendered, "[I will remain and continue] … so that" [cf. *Basics* 206; *ExSyn* 472].)

Philippians 1:27

- ἵνα (This is a purpose ἵνα clause related to πολιτεύεσθε. It can be rendered, "[I will remain and continue] … so that" [cf. *Basics* 206; *ExSyn* 472].)

- ἐλθών … ἰδών … ἀπών (These are conditional participles as is evident by the εἴτε that introduces them: "whether I come and see … or whether I am absent …")

18. πολιτεύεσθε: Voice, voice usage? [2+3]

- συναθλοῦντες (This is a participle of means related to στήκετε. It can be rendered "[you stand] by struggling together]" [cf. *Basics* 274-75; *ExSyn* 628-30].)

Philippians 1:28

19. πτυρόμενοι: Voice, voice usage? (This is a participle of means related to στήκετε.) [3+2]

_____

20. ἐν: Assuming that this preposition is used for agency, what type of agency is expressed by it? [2]

_____

21. ὑπό: What type of agency is expressed by this preposition? [2]

_____

22. ἀντικειμένων: Voice, voice usage? [2+2]

_____

- ἥτις (The reason this is feminine is not because of attraction to the gender of any previous word [such as ψυχή in v. 27] but because of attraction to the predicate nominative in its own clause, ἔνδειξις. When this phenomenon occurs, the emphasis is on the predicate nominative. See the discussion on Eph 1:13-14 in *ExSyn* 338.)

23. αὐτοῖς: Case, case usage, word related to? [1+1+1]

_____

24. ἀπωλείας: Case, case usage, word related to? [1+1+1]

_____

25. ὑμῶν: Case, case usage, word related to? [1+1+1]

_____

26. τοῦτο: What is the antecedent of this pronoun? Why is it neuter? [2+3]

_____

27. ἀπό: What type of agency is expressed by this preposition? [2]

_____

Philippians 1:29

- ὅτι (This is a causal ὅτι related to ἐστίν in 1:28. It can be rendered, "because" or "for" [cf. *Basics* 200–201; *ExSyn* 460–61].)

28. ἐχαρίσθη: Use of passive construction? [2]

_____

- τὸ ὑπὲρ Χριστοῦ (The article τό is substantiving the whole phrase ὑπὲρ Χριστοῦ, which is acting as the subject of ἐχαρίσθη. It can be woodenly rendered, "the things on behalf of Christ [have been granted to you]" [cf. *Basics* 105; *ExSyn* 236].)

- πιστεύειν … πάσχειν (These are appositional infinitives related to the phrase τὸ ὑπὲρ Χριστοῦ [cf. *Basics* 262–63; *ExSyn* 606–7].)

Lesson 10: Indicative Mood

Warm-Up Passages

Vocabulary

1. ἐμβλέπω : I look at, gaze on (Mt 6:26)	5. οὐράνιος : heavenly (Mt 6:26)
2. τὸ πετεινόν : bird (Mt 6:26)	6. τρέφω : I feed, nourish (Mt 6:26)
3. θερίζω : I harvest, reap (Mt 6:26)	7. διαφέρω : I carry through, spread; differ; to be worth more, be superior to (Mt 6:26)
4. ἡ ἀποθήκη : storehouse, barn (Mt 6:26)	

Luke 4:4

καὶ ἀπεκρίθη πρὸς αὐτὸν ὁ Ἰησοῦς· γέγραπται ὅτι οὐκ ἐπ᾽ ἄρτῳ μόνῳ ζήσεται ὁ ἄνθρωπος.

1. **ὅτι**: What is the usage of this ὅτι clause? [2]

_____

2. **ζήσεται**: If this verb is a declarative indicative, what does it mean? If it is a cohortative indicative, what does it mean? What do you think it is and why? [1+1+2]

_____

_____

Matthew 6:26

ἐμβλέψατε εἰς τὰ πετεινὰ τοῦ οὐρανοῦ ὅτι οὐ σπείρουσιν οὐδὲ θερίζουσιν οὐδὲ συνάγουσιν εἰς ἀποθήκας, καὶ ὁ πατὴρ ὑμῶν ὁ οὐράνιος τρέφει αὐτά· οὐχ ὑμεῖς μᾶλλον διαφέρετε αὐτῶν;

3. **ὅτι**: Classification of the ὅτι clause, word related to? [2+2]

_____

Syntax Passages

1 John 4:8-15

Background

In this section of the letter the motif of love is once again seen (cf. 3:11-14), only this time the emphasis is on sanctification more than assurance of salvation (4:7-21). This love is shown in Christ's death (4:7-12; cf. 3:16-17), which in turn is witnessed by the Spirit as a display of God's love (4:13-16a; cf. John 3:16). Once God's love is truly grasped—both by the evidence of history and the witness of the Spirit—it necessarily removes all fear, for "perfect love casts out fear" (4:16b-18).

Text

4:8 ὁ μὴ ἀγαπῶν οὐκ ἔγνω τὸν θεόν,
    ὅτι ὁ θεὸς ἀγάπη ἐστίν.
4:9 ἐν τούτῳ ἐφανερώθη ἡ ἀγάπη τοῦ θεοῦ ἐν ἡμῖν,
    ὅτι τὸν υἱὸν αὐτοῦ τὸν μονογενῆ ἀπέσταλκεν ὁ θεὸς
    εἰς τὸν κόσμον ἵνα ζήσωμεν δι᾽ αὐτοῦ.
4:10 ἐν τούτῳ ἐστὶν ἡ ἀγάπη,
    οὐχ ὅτι ἡμεῖς ἠγαπήκαμεν τὸν θεὸν
ἀλλ᾽ ὅτι αὐτὸς ἠγάπησεν ἡμᾶς
    καὶ ἀπέστειλεν τὸν υἱὸν αὐτοῦ
    ἱλασμὸν περὶ τῶν ἁμαρτιῶν ἡμῶν.

4:11 Ἀγαπητοί, εἰ οὕτως ὁ θεὸς ἠγάπησεν ἡμᾶς, καὶ ἡμεῖς ὀφείλομεν ἀλλήλους ἀγαπᾶν. **4:12** θεὸν οὐδεὶς πώποτε τεθέαται. ἐὰν ἀγαπῶμεν ἀλλήλους, ὁ θεὸς ἐν ἡμῖν μένει καὶ ἡ ἀγάπη αὐτοῦ ἐν ἡμῖν τετελειωμένη ἐστίν. **4:13** Ἐν τούτῳ γινώσκομεν ὅτι ἐν αὐτῷ μένομεν καὶ αὐτὸς ἐν ἡμῖν, ὅτι ἐκ τοῦ πνεύματος αὐτοῦ δέδωκεν ἡμῖν. **4:14** καὶ ἡμεῖς τεθεάμεθα καὶ μαρτυροῦμεν ὅτι ὁ πατὴρ ἀπέσταλκεν τὸν υἱὸν σωτῆρα τοῦ κόσμου. **4:15** Ὃς ἐὰν ὁμολογήσῃ ὅτι Ἰησοῦς ἐστιν ὁ υἱὸς τοῦ θεοῦ, ὁ θεὸς ἐν αὐτῷ μένει καὶ αὐτὸς ἐν τῷ θεῷ.

Vocabulary

1. φανερόω : I reveal, make known (v. 9)	6. θεάομαι : I see, look at (v. 12)
2. μονογενής : (one and) only; unique (in kind) (v. 9)	7. τελειόω : I complete, bring to an end; perfect (v. 12)
3. ὁ ἱλασμός : expiation, sacrifice to atone (v. 10)	8. ὁ σωτήρ : Savior, deliverer, preserver (v. 14)
4. ὀφείλω : I owe, am indebted (financial, social or moral sense); ought (v. 11)	9. ὁμολογέω : I promise; agree; confess; acknowledge (v. 15)
5. πώποτε : ever, at any time (v. 12)	

● 1 John 4:8

  4. ὅτι: Use of ὅτι clause, word related to? [1+2]

  _____

1 John 4:9

  • ὅτι (This conjunction is used to introduce an appositional clause. Such clauses are related
    to nouns, pronouns, or adjectives. In this case, the ὅτι clause refers back to (ἐν) τούτῳ.
    One way to see the connection is to read the ἐν τούτῳ as "in the following" [it is known
    as a cataphoric pronoun, referring to what follows], or to read it as "in the statement." If
    you think a ὅτι clause is functioning appositionally, you might try translating the ὅτι as
    "namely".)

  • ἵνα: (This is a ἵνα of purpose-result related to ἀπέστειλεν. It can be rendered, "[God sent
    his Son] … so that …" [cf. *Basics* 206-7; *ExSyn* 473-74].)

● 1 John 4:10

  5. ὅτι[1]: What is the usage of this ὅτι clause, and what does it modify? [2+2]

  _____

  6. ὅτι[2]: Use of ὅτι clause, word related to? [2+2]

  _____

1 John 4:11

  7. οὕτως: Name the specific use of this conjunction. [2]

  _____

  8. ἠγάπησεν: Mood, mood usage? [1+1]

  _____

● 9. ὀφείλομεν: Mood, mood usage? [1+2]

  _____

1 John 4:12

10. μένει: Mood, mood usage? [1+2]

_____

- τετελειωμένη (If this participle is periphrastic, the construction with ἐστίν is equivalent to a perfect indicative. It is also possible, though less likely, to treat the participle as a predicate adjective participle. Either way, the perfect tense still has its basic force of completed action with present results.)

1 John 4:13

11. ὅτι[1]: Use of ὅτι clause, word related to? [2+2]

_____

12. ὅτι[2]: Use of ὅτι clause, word related to? [2+2]

_____

1 John 4:14

13. ὅτι: Use of ὅτι clause, word related to? [2+2]

_____

14. σωτῆρα: Case, case usage, word related to? [1+1+1]

_____

1 John 4:15

15. ὅτι: Use of ὅτι clause, word related to? [2+2]

_____

John 8:17–20

Background

In this section of the Gospel of John, Jewish unbelief in spite of Jesus' teaching is addressed (7:1–8:59). Because the Jews were plotting to take Jesus' life, he went to the Feast of Tabernacles secretly (7:1, 11). Then, halfway through the feast, he began teaching publicly in the temple (7:14). The emphasis of his instruction was on a defense that he was from God (7:15–36) and that he was, in fact, God's Son (8:12–59).

Text

8:17 καὶ ἐν τῷ νόμῳ δὲ τῷ ὑμετέρῳ γέγραπται ὅτι δύο ἀνθρώπων ἡ μαρτυρία ἀληθής ἐστιν. **8:18** ἐγώ εἰμι ὁ μαρτυρῶν περὶ ἐμαυτοῦ καὶ μαρτυρεῖ περὶ ἐμοῦ ὁ πέμψας με πατήρ. **8:19** ἔλεγον οὖν αὐτῷ· ποῦ ἐστιν ὁ πατήρ σου; ἀπεκρίθη Ἰησοῦς· οὔτε ἐμὲ οἴδατε οὔτε τὸν πατέρα μου· εἰ ἐμὲ ᾔδειτε, καὶ τὸν πατέρα μου ἂν ᾔδειτε. **8:20** Ταῦτα τὰ ῥήματα ἐλάλησεν ἐν τῷ γαζοφυλακίῳ διδάσκων ἐν τῷ ἱερῷ· καὶ οὐδεὶς ἐπίασεν αὐτόν, ὅτι οὔπω ἐληλύθει ἡ ὥρα αὐτοῦ.

Vocabulary

1. ὑμέτερος : your (pl.) (v. 17)	6. ᾔδειτε : plupft. of οἶδα (v. 19)
2. μαρτυρία : testimony, witness, reputation (v. 17)	7. τὸ γαζοφυλάκιον : treasure room, treasury; contribution box (v. 20)
3. ἀληθής : truthful, righteous (v. 17)	8. πιάζω : I grasp, take (hold of) (v. 20)
4. ἐμαυτοῦ : (of) myself (v. 18)	9. οὔπω : not yet (v. 20)
5. ποῦ : where? (v. 19)	

John 8:17

16. **ὅτι**: The introduction of the ὅτι clause after γέγραπται suggests that the ὅτι clause may be functioning to introduce direct discourse. (Your Greek NT will give you sufficient clues as to whether this is the case or whether it is introducing indirect discourse. The UBS[4] will give one clue and the Nestle-Aland[27] will give another.) Is this introducing direct discourse or indirect discourse? Support your answer with evidence supplied from both Greek NTs (UBS and NA) and the LXX. [2+4]

_____

_____

_____

John 8:19

- ἔλεγον (This may be an ingressive imperfect, which "is often used to stress the beginning of an action, with the implication that it continued for some time" [*ExSyn* 544; cf. *Basics* 233, *ExSyn* 544-45], or it could be an instantaneous imperfect in which the accent is on the vividness of what was said ["The imperfect is often the tense of choice to introduce such *vivid* sayings. In this respect, it parallels the historical (dramatic) present" [*ExSyn* 542].)

17. ἐστιν: Mood, mood usage? [1+2]

_____

18. ᾔδειτε: Mood, mood usage? [1+2]

_____

John 8:20

- διδάσκων (This is a temporal participle of contemporaneous time related to ἐλάλησεν. It can be rendered, "[He spoke these words] ... while he was teaching ..." [cf. *Basics* 272-73; *ExSyn* 623-27].)

19. ὅτι: Use of ὅτι clause, word related to? [2+2]

_____

John 9:27, 30-35

Background

John 9:1-10:39 addresses Jewish unbelief in spite of Jesus' healing of a blind man. This was a healing on the Sabbath (9:13-16), and for this very reason the Jews refused to believe that Jesus was sent from God (9:16). We pick up the narrative with the formerly blind man arguing with the religious authorities about who and what Jesus was.

Text

9:27 ἀπεκρίθη αὐτοῖς· εἶπον ὑμῖν ἤδη καὶ οὐκ ἠκούσατε· τί πάλιν θέλετε ἀκούειν; μὴ καὶ ὑμεῖς θέλετε αὐτοῦ μαθηταὶ γενέσθαι; ... **9:30** ἀπεκρίθη ὁ ἄνθρωπος καὶ εἶπεν αὐτοῖς· ἐν τούτῳ γὰρ τὸ θαυμαστόν ἐστιν, ὅτι ὑμεῖς οὐκ οἴδατε πόθεν ἐστίν, καὶ ἤνοιξέν μου τοὺς ὀφθαλμούς. **9:31** οἴδαμεν ὅτι ἁμαρτωλῶν ὁ θεὸς οὐκ ἀκούει, ἀλλ' ἐάν τις θεοσεβὴς ᾖ καὶ τὸ θέλημα αὐτοῦ ποιῇ τούτου ἀκούει. **9:32** ἐκ τοῦ αἰῶνος οὐκ ἠκούσθη ὅτι ἠνέῳξέν τις ὀφθαλμοὺς τυφλοῦ γεγεννημένου· **9:33** εἰ μὴ ἦν οὗτος παρὰ θεοῦ, οὐκ ἠδύνατο ποιεῖν οὐδέν. **9:34** ἀπεκρίθησαν καὶ εἶπαν αὐτῷ· ἐν ἁμαρτίαις σὺ ἐγεννήθης ὅλος καὶ σὺ διδάσκεις ἡμᾶς; καὶ ἐξέβαλον αὐτὸν ἔξω.

9:35 Ἤκουσεν Ἰησοῦς ὅτι ἐξέβαλον αὐτὸν ἔξω καὶ εὑρὼν αὐτὸν εἶπεν, σὺ πιστεύεις εἰς τὸν υἱὸν τοῦ ἀνθρώπου;

Vocabulary

1. θαυμαστός : wonderful, marvelous (v. 30)	3. ἁμαρτωλός : sinful, sinner (v. 31)
2. πόθεν : from where; from what source (v. 30)	4. θεοσεβής : God-fearing, devout (v. 31)

John 9:27

20. **θέλετε**[1]: Mood, mood usage? [1+2]

_____

_____

- **μή** (Questions expecting the answer "no" are usually introduced with μή [Moule, *Idiom Book*[2], 159].)

21. **θέλετε**[2]: Mood, mood usage? [1+2]

_____

John 9:30

22. **ὅτι**: What is the usage of this ὅτι clause? What word is it related to? [2+2]

_____

23. **ἤνοιξεν**: Voice, voice usage, word related to? [1+2+2]

_____

John 9:31

24. ὅτι: Use of ὅτι clause, word related to? [2+2]

_____

• ἐάν (This conjunction is introducing a third class condition. These conditional clauses often present "the condition as uncertain of fulfillment, but still likely" [*ExSyn* 696; cf. *Basics* 313, *ExSyn* 696–99].)

John 9:32

25. ὅτι: Use of ὅτι clause, word related to? [2+2]

_____

John 9:33

• εἰ (This conjunction is introducing a second class condition. These conditional clauses indicate the "assumption of an untruth (for the sake of argument)" [*ExSyn* 694; cf. *Basics* 312; *ExSyn* 694–96]. They are of two types: present contrary-to-fact and past contrary-to-fact. The present contrary-to-fact conditions use imperfects in the protasis and apodosis; the past contrary-to-fact condition uses aorists. The following two sentences illustrate the differences in translation between these two: If X were ... then Y would be [as in "If you were a good man, then you would not be here right now."]. This is present contrary-to-fact. Or consider: If X had been ... then Y would have been [as in "If you had been here yesterday, you would have seen a great game."].)

26. ἦν: What *specific* type of conditional clause is this verb in? How should the whole verse be translated in light of your decision? [2+2]

_____

_____

John 9:34

27. ὅλος: Check usage in BDAG for this specific passage; give their gloss in this context. [2]

_____

● John 9:35

28. ὅτι: Use of ὅτι clause, word related to? [2+2]

_____

29. πιστεύεις: Mood, mood usage? [1+2]

_____

- τοῦ ἀνθρώπου (The majority of MSS actually read θεοῦ here instead of ἀνθρώπου, although ἀνθρώπου has the better witnesses on its side [P⁶⁶, ⁷⁵ ℵ B D W syrˢ copˢᵃ al]. ἀνθρώπου also has better internal evidence: it is highly unlikely that a scribe would change θεοῦ to ἀνθρώπου, but a scribe might be tempted to the opposite change in order to heighten reference to Jesus' deity in this passage.)

Lesson 11: Subjunctive Mood

Warm-Up Passages

Vocabulary

1. ὁ γεωργός : farmer, vine-dresser (Mt 21:38)	5. ἐπιμένω : I stay, remain, continue (Ro 6:1)
2. ὁ κληρονόμος : heir, beneficiary (Mt 21:38)	6. πλεονάζω : I become more, grow, increase (Ro 6:1)
3. δεῦτε : come, come here (Mt 21:38)	7. δικαιόω : I justify, vindicate (Ro 5:1)
4. ἡ κληρονομία : inheritance, possession (Mt 21:38)	

Matthew 21:38

οἱ δὲ γεωργοὶ ἰδόντες τὸν υἱὸν εἶπον ἐν ἑαυτοῖς· οὗτός ἐστιν ὁ κληρονόμος· δεῦτε ἀποκτείνωμεν αὐτὸν καὶ σχῶμεν τὴν κληρονομίαν αὐτοῦ.

1. **ἐν**: How is this preposition being used here? What is the best translation in this context? See BDAG, ἐν 1.d for help. [1+1]

_____

2. **ἀποκτείνωμεν**: Mood, mood usage? [1+2]

_____

3. **σχῶμεν**: Mood, mood usage? [2+2]

_____

Romans 6:1

Τί οὖν ἐροῦμεν; ἐπιμένωμεν τῇ ἁμαρτίᾳ, ἵνα ἡ χάρις πλεονάσῃ;

4. **ἐπιμένωμεν**: Mood, mood usage? [1+2]

_____

5. ἐπιμένωμεν: One textual variant for ἐπιμένωμεν is ἐπιμενοῦμεν. What mood is this and what is the mood's usage? [2+2]

---

6. ἵνα: Use of ἵνα clause, word related to? [1+2]

Romans 5:1

Δικαιωθέντες οὖν ἐκ πίστεως εἰρήνην ἔχομεν πρὸς τὸν θεὸν διὰ τοῦ κυρίου ἡμῶν Ἰησοῦ Χριστοῦ.

- **Δικαιωθέντες** (This is a participle of cause related to ἔχομεν. It can be rendered, "because we are justified" [cf. *Basics* 275-76; *ExSyn* 631-32].)

7. ἐκ ... πρός ... διά: It has been observed that the vitality of a religion is found in its use of prepositions. Without these three prepositional phrases this verse would only be rendered "having been justified, we have peace." How are these three prepositions functioning and what important information do they add to this verse? [1+1+1]

---

8. ἔχομεν: (There is an interesting textual variant for this word. Several important MSS have the subjunctive ἔχωμεν [e.g., ℵ* A B* C D 33 81]. The indicative reading [ἔχομεν] has weaker external support [ℵ¹ B² F G Ψ 0220ᵛⁱᵈ], although the oldest MS for this passage, 0220, apparently attests it. Thus the external evidence does seem to favor the subjunctive reading and the "A" rating that the UBS committee granted the indicative reading appears to be too optimistic. However, textual critics have noted that the indicative is more appropriate for the context of Romans and thus it should be favored.) Why is the indicative considered more appropriate here? (Try to consult at least one exegetical commentary on this passage.) How would the subjunctive change the meaning of the text? Supposing ἔχωμεν is the correct reading, what is its mood usage? [3+2+2]

Syntax Passages

Matthew 5:13–19

Background

The Sermon on the Mount begins with a focus on the character that Jesus demanded of his disciples, of those who would be part of the kingdom of God (5:3-16). Before he lists any responsibilities for them, however, Jesus first motivates his audience to see the wealth of character (as opposed to the wealth of material possessions), heading the list with those who are "poor in spirit" (5:3). Essentially those who live for God are blessed (5:3-12). They also have a responsibility to let their "salt" and "light" have their impact on society (5:13-16).

After this brief exposition about the members of the kingdom, Jesus gives several truths about the nature of the kingdom itself (5:17-7:12). These again focus on character development, with a strong emphasis on internal righteousness in an externally ugly world. This is the major section of the sermon, and it is no accident that Jesus begins by linking his views with those of the OT prophets—that is, by giving an exposition of the *intent* of the OT law (5:17-48). Arguably the core of the entire Sermon on the Mount is at the front-end of this exposition, for Jesus affirms that the principles of the OT law are inviolable (5:17-20).

Text

5:13 Ὑμεῖς ἐστε τὸ ἅλας τῆς γῆς· ἐὰν δὲ τὸ ἅλας μωρανθῇ, ἐν τίνι ἁλισθήσεται; εἰς οὐδὲν ἰσχύει ἔτι εἰ μὴ βληθὲν ἔξω καταπατεῖσθαι ὑπὸ τῶν ἀνθρώπων.

5:14 Ὑμεῖς ἐστε τὸ φῶς τοῦ κόσμου. οὐ δύναται πόλις κρυβῆναι ἐπάνω ὄρους κειμένη· **5:15** οὐδὲ καίουσιν λύχνον καὶ τιθέασιν αὐτὸν ὑπὸ τὸν μόδιον ἀλλ᾽ ἐπὶ τὴν λυχνίαν, καὶ λάμπει πᾶσιν τοῖς ἐν τῇ οἰκίᾳ. **5:16** οὕτως λαμψάτω τὸ φῶς ὑμῶν ἔμπροσθεν τῶν ἀνθρώπων, ὅπως ἴδωσιν ὑμῶν τὰ καλὰ ἔργα καὶ δοξάσωσιν τὸν πατέρα ὑμῶν τὸν ἐν τοῖς οὐρανοῖς.

5:17 Μὴ νομίσητε ὅτι ἦλθον καταλῦσαι τὸν νόμον ἢ τοὺς προφήτας· οὐκ ἦλθον καταλῦσαι ἀλλὰ πληρῶσαι. **5:18** ἀμὴν γὰρ λέγω ὑμῖν· ἕως ἂν παρέλθῃ ὁ οὐρανὸς καὶ ἡ γῆ, ἰῶτα ἓν ἢ μία κεραία οὐ μὴ παρέλθῃ ἀπὸ τοῦ νόμου, ἕως ἂν πάντα γένηται. **5:19** ὃς ἐὰν οὖν λύσῃ μίαν τῶν ἐντολῶν τούτων τῶν ἐλαχίστων καὶ διδάξῃ οὕτως τοὺς ἀνθρώπους, ἐλάχιστος κληθήσεται ἐν τῇ βασιλείᾳ τῶν οὐρανῶν· ὃς δ᾽ ἂν ποιήσῃ καὶ διδάξῃ, οὗτος μέγας κληθήσεται ἐν τῇ βασιλείᾳ τῶν οὐρανῶν.

Vocabulary

1. τὸ ἅλας : salt (v. 13)	12. ἡ λυχνία : lampstand (v. 15)
2. μωραίνω : I make foolish; make tasteless (v. 13)	13. λάμπω : I shine, light (v. 15)
3. ἁλίζω : I salt, am made salty (pass.) (v. 13)	14. ἔμπροσθεν : before, in front, ahead (v. 16)
4. ἰσχύω : I be in good health, be healthy (v. 13)	15. νομίζω : I think, believe, consider (v. 17)

5. καταπατέω : I trample (under foot), tread upon (v. 13)	16. καταλύω : I throw down; destroy (v. 17)
6. κρύπτω : I hide, keep secret (v. 14)	17. παρέρχομαι : I go or pass by; pass away (v. 18)
7. ἐπάνω : above, over (lit. and fig.) (v. 14)	18. τὸ ἰῶτα : iota (v. 18)
8. κεῖμαι : I lie, recline (v. 14)	19. ἡ κεραία : serif (part of a letter); hook (v. 18)
9. καίω : I light, have or keep burning (v. 15)	20. λύω : I loose, untie, set free; abolish, destroy; allow (v. 19)
10. ὁ λύχνος lamp (lit. and fig.) (v. 15)	21. ἐλάχιστος : least, smallest, unimportant (v. 19)
11. ὁ μόδιος container (for measuring grain, holds about 8.75 liters or 8 quarts) (v. 15)	

Matthew 5:13

9. **μωρανθῇ**: Mood, mood usage? [1+2]

_____

10. **εἰ μή**: Look up εἰ in BDAG, under definition 6. What gloss does BDAG give to this phrase as it is used in Matt 5:13? [2]

_____

- **βληθέν** (This is a complementary participle related to ἰσχύει. Complementary participles complete the thought of another verb [*ExSyn* 646]. It can be rendered "[it is good for nothing except] to be cast out." Typically the verb ἰσχύω takes a complementary *infinitive* [see BDAG, s.v. ἰσχύω 2.b], but here and in one other place in the New Testament it takes the participle [cf. Jas 5:15].)

- **καταπατεῖσθαι** (This is an infinitive of result related to βληθέν. It can be rendered, "[to be cast out] with the result that it is trampled on" [cf. *Basics* 257-58; *ExSyn* 592-94].)

Matthew 5:14

- **κρυβῆναι** (This is a complementary infinitive related to δύναται [cf. *Basics* 259-60; *ExSyn* 598-99].)

11. κρυβῆναι: Voice, use of voice? [1+2]

_____

Matthew 5:16

- ἴδωσιν: This subjunctive is in a dependent clause introduced by ὅπως. This conjunction often functions like ἵνα, introducing a purpose clause.

12. δοξάσωσιν: Mood, mood usage, word related to? [1+2+2]

_____

13. τόν²: Usage of the article (do not treat as function marker)? [2]

_____

Matthew 5:17

14. νομίσητε: Mood, mood usage? [1+2]

_____

- καταλῦσαι (This is an infinitive of purpose related to ἦλθον. It can be rendered, "[Do not think that I came] for the purpose of destroying" [cf. *Basics* 256-57; *ExSyn* 590-92].)

Matthew 5:18

15. παρέλθῃ¹: Mood, mood usage? [1+2]

_____

16. παρέλθῃ²: Mood, mood usage? [1+2]

_____

17. γένηται: Mood, mood usage, word related to? [1+2]

_____

● Matthew 5:19

18. διδάξῃ¹: Mood, mood usage? [1+2]

_____

19. ποιήσῃ: Mood, mood usage? [1+2]

_____

20. κληθήσεται: Mood, use of mood? [1+2]

_____

John 11:49–57

Background

In this section of John's Gospel, the religious leaders solidified their plot against Jesus' life. In their latest confrontation, Jesus raised a man from the dead (10:40–11:44), causing many Jews ● finally to believe in him (11:45). The Sanhedrin consequently planned to take his life, out of political and religious expediency (11:48). Unwittingly, the high priest speaks better than he knows when he argues for the necessity of Jesus' death (11:50). The evangelist capitalizes on this (11:51–52), then notes that Jesus went into hiding while the religious leaders began looking for him (11:53–57).

Text

11:49 εἷς δέ τις ἐξ αὐτῶν Καϊάφας, ἀρχιερεὺς ὢν τοῦ ἐνιαυτοῦ ἐκείνου, εἶπεν αὐτοῖς· ὑμεῖς οὐκ οἴδατε οὐδέν, **11:50** οὐδὲ λογίζεσθε ὅτι συμφέρει ὑμῖν ἵνα εἷς ἄνθρωπος ἀποθάνῃ ὑπὲρ τοῦ λαοῦ καὶ μὴ ὅλον τὸ ἔθνος ἀπόληται. **11:51** τοῦτο δὲ ἀφ' ἑαυτοῦ οὐκ εἶπεν, ἀλλὰ ἀρχιερεὺς ὢν τοῦ ἐνιαυτοῦ ἐκείνου ἐπροφήτευσεν ὅτι ἔμελλεν Ἰησοῦς ἀποθνήσκειν ὑπὲρ τοῦ ἔθνους, **11:52** καὶ οὐχ ὑπὲρ τοῦ ἔθνους μόνον ἀλλ' ἵνα καὶ τὰ τέκνα τοῦ θεοῦ τὰ διεσκορπισμένα συναγάγῃ εἰς ἕν. **11:53** ἀπ' ἐκείνης οὖν τῆς ἡμέρας ἐβουλεύσαντο ἵνα ἀποκτείνωσιν αὐτόν.

11:54 Ὁ οὖν Ἰησοῦς οὐκέτι παρρησίᾳ περιεπάτει ἐν τοῖς Ἰουδαίοις, ἀλλὰ ἀπῆλθεν ἐκεῖθεν εἰς τὴν χώραν ἐγγὺς τῆς ἐρήμου, εἰς Ἐφραὶμ λεγομένην πόλιν, κἀκεῖ ἔμεινεν μετὰ τῶν μαθητῶν.

11:55 Ἦν δὲ ἐγγὺς τὸ πάσχα τῶν Ἰουδαίων, καὶ ἀνέβησαν πολλοὶ εἰς Ἱεροσόλυμα ἐκ τῆς χώρας πρὸ τοῦ πάσχα ἵνα ἁγνίσωσιν ἑαυτούς. **11:56** ἐζήτουν οὖν τὸν Ἰησοῦν καὶ ἔλεγον μετ' ἀλλήλων ἐν τῷ ἱερῷ ἑστηκότες· τί δοκεῖ ὑμῖν; ὅτι οὐ μὴ ἔλθῃ εἰς τὴν ἑορτήν; **11:57** δεδώκεισαν δὲ οἱ ἀρχιερεῖς καὶ οἱ Φαρισαῖοι ἐντολὰς ἵνα ἐάν τις γνῷ ποῦ ἐστιν μηνύσῃ, ὅπως πιάσωσιν αὐτόν.

Vocabulary

1. ὁ Καϊάφας : Caiaphas (v. 49)	13. ἡ ἔρημος : desolate; desert, wilderness (v. 54)
2. ὁ ἐνιαυτός : year (v. 49)	14. ὁ Ἐφραίμ : Ephraim (v. 54)
3. λογίζομαι : I calculate, consider ponder (v. 50)	15. κἀκεῖ : and there, there also (v. 54)
4. συμφέρω : I bring together; it is better (impers.) (v. 50)	16. πρό : before, in front of, ahead (v. 55)
5. προφητεύω : I prophesy, tell, reveal (v. 51)	17. τὸ πάσχα : Passover (v. 55)
6. διασκορπίζω : I scatter, disperse v. 52)	18. ἁγνίζω : I purify, cleanse (v. 55)
7. βουλεύω : I deliberate, resolve, decide (mid in NT) (v. 53)	19. ἡ ἑορτή : festival, celebration (v. 56)
8. οὐκέτι no longer : (v. 54)	20. δεδώκεισαν : plupft. of δίδωμι (v. 57)
9. παρρησία : outspoken, frankness; confidence, boldness (v. 54)	21. ποῦ : where? (v. 57)
10. ἐκεῖθεν : from there (v. 54)	22. γνῷ : 2 aor. subj. of γινώσκω (v. 57)
11. ἡ χώρα : land, district, region (v. 54)	23. μηνύω : I make reknown, reveal, inform (v. 57)
12. ἐγγύς : near, close (v. 54)	24. πιάζω : I grasp, take (hold of), seize (v. 57)

John 11:50

- ὑμῖν (Although several MSS have ἡμῖν [A W Δ Θ Ψ 0141 0250], the reading in the text should be retained because it has better external support [P⁴⁵, ⁶⁶ B D L 0233 1010 1241] and because scribes might have been tempted to change ὑμῖν to ἡμῖν to emphasize the culpability of the high priest in Jesus' death.)

21. ἵνα: Use of ἵνα clause, word related to? [2+2]

22. ὑπέρ: Read the treatment on ὑπέρ in *Basics* 171-73; *ExSyn* 383-89. What is the force of ὑπέρ here? Why is this example significant? [2+2]

● John 11:51

- ὤν (This is a participle of cause related to εἶπεν. It can be rendered, "because he was [high priest that year]" [cf. *Basics* 275-76; *ExSyn* 631-32].)

- ἀποθνῄσκειν (This is a complementary infinitive related to ἔμελλεν. [cf. *Basics* 259-60; *ExSyn* 598-99].)

John 11:52

23. ἵνα: Use of ἵνα clause, word related to? [1+2]

_____

John 11:53

24. ἵνα: Use of ἵνα clause, word related to? [2+2]

● _____

John 11:55

25. ἵνα: Use of ἵνα clause, word related to? [1+2]

_____

John 11:56

- ἑστηκότες (This is a temporal participle of contemporaneous time related to ἔλεγον. Such is unusual for a perfect participle, but in this case the perfect verb ἕστηκα is customarily a perfect with present force. Thus, it functions like a present participle. It can be rendered "[they were saying to one another] while they were standing [in the temple]" [cf. *Basics* 272-73; *ExSyn* 623-27].)

26. ἔλθῃ: Mood, mood usage? [1+2]

● _____

John 11:57

27. οἱ ἀρχιερεῖς καὶ οἱ Φαρισαῖοι: If the second article were absent, what kind of construction would this be? What semantic category would it belong to? (See "Article, Part II" in *Basics* or *ExSyn* for help.) [2+2]

---

28. ἵνα: Use of ἵνα clause, word related to? [2+2]

---

29. γνῷ: Mood, mood usage? [1+2]

- μηνύσῃ (This subjunctive verb is part of a very complicated construction. This verb is in the apodosis of a third class conditional clause, which is embedded within a ἵνα clause. The conditional clause [ἐάν τις γνῷ ποῦ ἐστιν μηνύσῃ] can be translated "if anyone knew where he was, he should make (this) known." The reason the subjunctive verbs are translated like past tense verbs is because the ἵνα clause also functions like indirect discourse, picking up the implication of implied speech from ἐντολάς. Thus, we have an embedded conditional clause inside a ἵνα clause that is doing double duty as introducing indirect discourse!)

30. πιάσωσιν: Mood, mood usage? [1+2]

Lesson 12: Optative and Imperative Moods

Warm-Up Passage

Vocabulary

1. ὑποτάσσω : I subject, bring to subjection (v. 7)	6. καθαρίζω : I make clean; heal (v. 8)
2. ἀνθίστημι : I oppose; resist (v. 7)	7. ὁ ἁμαρτωλός : sinner (v. 8)
3. ὁ διάβολος : the devil (subst.) (v. 7)	8. ἁγνίζω : I purify, cleanse (v. 8)
4. φεύγω : I flee; escape (v. 7)	9. δίψυχος : double-minded (lit.), doubting (v. 8)
5. ἐγγίζω : I draw near; approach (v. 8)	

James 4:7–8

4:7 ὑποτάγητε οὖν τῷ θεῷ, ἀντίστητε δὲ τῷ διαβόλῳ καὶ φεύξεται ἀφ᾽ ὑμῶν, **4:8** ἐγγίσατε τῷ θεῷ καὶ ἐγγιεῖ ὑμῖν. καθαρίσατε χεῖρας, ἁμαρτωλοί, καὶ ἁγνίσατε καρδίας, δίψυχοι.

1. **ὑποτάγητε**: Mood, mood usage? [2+2]

_____

2. **ἀντίστητε**: Mood, mood usage? [1+2]

_____

3. **ἐγγίσατε**: Mood, mood usage? [2+2]

_____

4. **ἐγγιεῖ**: Mood, mood usage? [2+2]

_____

5. **καθαρίσατε**: Mood, mood usage? [1+2]

_____

6. ἁμαρτωλοί: Case, case usage, word related to? [1+2+1]

_____

7. ἁγνίσατε: Mood, mood usage? [1+2]

_____

Syntax Passages

Matthew 14:27-30

Background

In the midst of Jesus' withdrawals from the crowds and from danger (13:54-16:20), he still performs miracles (feeding the five thousand [14:13-21], walks on the water [14:22-33], and heals the sick at Gennesaret [14:34-36]).

Text

14:27 εὐθὺς δὲ ἐλάλησεν ὁ Ἰησοῦς αὐτοῖς λέγων· θαρσεῖτε, ἐγώ εἰμι, μὴ φοβεῖσθε. **14:28** ἀποκριθεὶς δὲ αὐτῷ ὁ Πέτρος εἶπεν· κύριε, εἰ σὺ εἶ, κέλευσόν με ἐλθεῖν πρός σε ἐπὶ τὰ ὕδατα. **14:29** ὁ δὲ εἶπεν· ἐλθέ. καὶ καταβὰς ἀπὸ τοῦ πλοίου ὁ Πέτρος περιεπάτησεν ἐπὶ τὰ ὕδατα καὶ ἦλθεν πρὸς τὸν Ἰησοῦν. **14:30** βλέπων δὲ τὸν ἄνεμον ἰσχυρὸν ἐφοβήθη, καὶ ἀρξάμενος καταποντίζεσθαι ἔκραξεν λέγων· κύριε, σῶσον με.

Vocabulary

1. θαρσέω : I am courageous; have courage! (only impv. in NT) (v. 27)	4. ἰσχυρός : strong; violent (v. 30)
2. κελεύω : I command, order, urge (v. 28)	5. καταποντίζω : I drown; am sunk (pass. in NT) (v. 30)
3. ὁ ἄνεμος : wind (v. 30)	

Matthew 14:27

8. θαρσεῖτε: Mood, mood usage? [1+2]

_____

9. φοβεῖσθε: Mood, mood usage? [2+2]

_____

Matthew 14:28

- ἀποκριθείς (This is a redundant participle; it refers to the same action as the verb it modifies, εἶπεν.)

10. κέλευσον: Mood, mood usage? [1+2]

_____

- ἐλθεῖν (This is an indirect discourse infinitive related to κέλευσον. These infinitives are used "after a verb of *perception* or *communication*" [cf. *Basics* 261; *ExSyn* 603–5]. It could be rendered, "[Command me] to come.")

Matthew 14:29

11. ὁ¹: Use of article? What clues are there in the context that this is so? [2+2]

_____

_____

12. ἐλθέ: Mood, mood usage? [1+2]

_____

- καταβάς (This is an attendant circumstance participle related to περιεπάτησεν.)

- περιεπάτησεν (This aorist most likely has an ingressive force here: "[Peter] began to walk [on the water]." It finds its culmination in the next aorist verb.)

- ἦλθεν (This aorist has a consummative force: "[Peter began to walk on the water and] came [to Jesus].")

Matthew 14:30

- βλέπων (This is a temporal participle of antecedent or contemporaneous time related to ἐφοβήθη. It could be rendered, "[after/when] he saw" [cf. *Basics* 272–73; *ExSyn* 623–27].)

- ἰσχυρόν (Several MSS have just the reading ἄνεμον [א B* 073 33 vg^ms cop^{sa, bo, fay}], while others also have, after ἄνεμον, the adjective ἰσχυρόν [B² C D L Δ Θ 0106]. At first glance ἰσχυρόν could be seen as a scribal addition to add some color to the narrative. But the simple reading of ἄνεμον lacks geographical distribution among those text-types; that is, it is only represented by the Alexandrian text-type [Metzger, *Textual Commentary*², 30]. A decision is thus difficult: the Alexandrian text is to be preferred, but the lack of geographical distribution makes the external evidence less than certain. The "C" rating in the UBS text is justified.)

13. ἰσχυρον: Position of adjective, word related to? Translate this word with the word it is related to in order to bring out its syntactical force. [2+1+3]

- ἀρξάμενος (This is a temporal participle of antecedent or contemporaneous time. It is related to ἔκραξεν. Aorist participles are usually antecedent to the verb on which they depend. However, when the verb is also aorist, they are often contemporaneous. In many instances, the time of the participle is so close to the time of the verb that it makes little difference whether it is called antecedent or contemporaneous. So here: presumably, the time for Peter to sink would not be too drawn out!)

- καταποντίζεσθαι (This is a complementary infinitive related to ἀρξάμενος. These infinitives help complete the thought of another verbal idea. It can be rendered, "[when he began] to sink" [cf. *Basics* 259–60; *ExSyn* 598–99].)

14. σῶσον: Mood, mood usage? [1+2]

Romans 11:9–12

Background

Will Israel persist in their disobedience, or will there come a time when they will repent? Paul answers this in Romans 11. He points out, first, that God's rejection of the nation is not complete, for God still has his remnant in the nation (11:1–10). Further, the rejection is not final (11:11–32). Indeed, the present "grafting in" of Gentiles not only functions to bring salvation to Gentiles, but also should arouse the jealousy of the Jews, hopefully even spurring them on to seek Christ (11:11–24).

Text

11:9 καὶ Δαυὶδ λέγει·
γενηθήτω ἡ τράπεζα αὐτῶν εἰς παγίδα καὶ εἰς θήραν
    καὶ εἰς σκάνδαλον καὶ εἰς ἀνταπόδομα αὐτοῖς,
11:10 σκοτισθήτωσαν οἱ ὀφθαλμοὶ αὐτῶν τοῦ μὴ βλέπειν
    καὶ τὸν νῶτον αὐτῶν διὰ παντὸς σύγκαμψον.

11:11 Λέγω οὖν, μὴ ἔπταισαν ἵνα πέσωσιν; μὴ γένοιτο· ἀλλὰ τῷ αὐτῶν παραπτώματι ἡ σωτηρία τοῖς ἔθνεσιν εἰς τὸ παραζηλῶσαι αὐτούς. **11:12** εἰ δὲ τὸ παράπτωμα αὐτῶν πλοῦτος κόσμου καὶ τὸ ἥττημα αὐτῶν πλοῦτος ἐθνῶν, πόσῳ μᾶλλον τὸ πλήρωμα αὐτῶν.

Vocabulary

1. ἡ τράπεζα : table; meal (v. 9)	10. πταίω : I stumble, sin (v. 11)
2. ἡ παγίς : trap, snare (lit. and fig.) (v. 9)	11. τὸ παράπτωμα : offense, sin (v. 11)
3. ἡ θήρα : net, trap (v. 9)	12. ἡ σωτηρία : deliverance; salvation (v. 11)
4. τὸ σκάνδαλον : trap; enticement; stumbling-block (v. 9)	13. παραζηλόω : I provoke to jealousy, make jealous (v. 11)
5. τὸ ἀνταπόδομα : reward; recompense (v. 9)	14. ὁ, τὸ πλοῦτος : riches, wealth; abundance (v. 12)
6. σκοτίζω : I am darkened (pass. in NT) (v. 10)	15. τὸ ἥττημα : loss (v. 12)
7. ὁ νῶτος : back (of the body) (v. 10)	16. πόσος : how great, how much (v. 12)
8. διὰ παντός : forever (v. 10)	17. τὸ πλήρωμα : that which fills (up); fullness (v. 12)
9. συγκάμπτω : I (cause to) bend (v. 10)	

Romans 11:9

15. **γενηθήτω**: Look up Ps 69:23-24, which is being quoted here (68:23-24 in the LXX). How is this imperative being used in that context? Is Paul using it in the same way? [3+3]

Romans 11:10

16. **σκοτισθήτωσαν**: Mood, mood usage? [1+2]

- βλέπειν (This is an infinitive of result related to σκοτισθήτωσαν. It could be rendered, "[Let their eyes be darkened] with the result that they cannot see" [cf. *Basics* 257-58; *ExSyn* 592-94].)

17. σύγκαμψον: Mood, mood usage? [1+2]

_____

18. σύγκαμψον: Voice, voice usage? [1+2]

_____

Romans 11:11

- μή[1] (Questions prefaced by μή expect a negative answer.)

19. ἵνα: What is the usage of this ἵνα clause? [3]

_____

20. γένοιτο: Mood, mood usage? [2+2]

_____

- παραζηλῶσαι (This is an infinitive of purpose or possibly result related to an implied εἰμί. It could be rendered, "[Salvation is to the Gentiles] {in order to make/with the result of making} [the Jews] jealous" [cf. *Basics* 256-57; *ExSyn* 590-92].)

Romans 11:12

21. πόσῳ: What type of pronoun is this? What is the basic difference between πόσος and ποῖος? [2+2]

_____

Matthew 8:21-27

Background

After a brief statement about the cost of discipleship (8:18-22), a group of miracles are performed, demonstrating Jesus' authority in the realm of nature (calming the storm, 8:23-27), in the realm of the supernatural (healing the two Gadarene demoniacs, 8:28-34), and even in the realm of the spiritual (healing a paralytic along with the forgiveness of his sins, 9:1-8).

Text

8:21 ἕτερος δὲ τῶν μαθητῶν αὐτοῦ εἶπεν αὐτῷ· κύριε, ἐπίτρεψόν μοι πρῶτον ἀπελθεῖν καὶ θάψαι τὸν πατέρα μου. **8:22** ὁ δὲ Ἰησοῦς λέγει αὐτῷ· ἀκολούθει μοι καὶ ἄφες τοὺς νεκροὺς θάψαι τοὺς ἑαυτῶν νεκρούς.

8:23 Καὶ ἐμβάντι αὐτῷ εἰς τὸ πλοῖον ἠκολούθησαν αὐτῷ οἱ μαθηταὶ αὐτοῦ. **8:24** καὶ ἰδοὺ σεισμὸς μέγας ἐγένετο ἐν τῇ θαλάσσῃ, ὥστε τὸ πλοῖον καλύπτεσθαι ὑπὸ τῶν κυμάτων, αὐτὸς δὲ ἐκάθευδεν. **8:25** καὶ προσελθόντες ἤγειραν αὐτὸν λέγοντες· κύριε, σῶσον, ἀπολλύμεθα. **8:26** καὶ λέγει αὐτοῖς· τί δειλοί ἐστε, ὀλιγόπιστοι; τότε ἐγερθεὶς ἐπετίμησεν τοῖς ἀνέμοις καὶ τῇ θαλάσσῃ, καὶ ἐγένετο γαλήνη μεγάλη. **8:27** οἱ δὲ ἄνθρωποι ἐθαύμασαν λέγοντες· ποταπός ἐστιν οὗτος ὅτι καὶ οἱ ἄνεμοι καὶ ἡ θάλασσα αὐτῷ ὑπακούουσιν;

Vocabulary

1. ἐπιτρέπω : I allow, permit (v. 21)	9. ὀλιγόπιστος : of little faith or trust (v. 26)
2. θάπτω : I bury (v. 21)	10. ἐπιτιμάω : I rebuke, censure (v. 26)
3. ἐμβαίνω : I embark; step into, go on board (v. 23)	11. ὁ ἄνεμος : wind
4. ὁ σεισμός : earthquake; storm (on a body of water) (v. 24)	12. ἡ γαλήνη : calm (of a body of water) (v. 26)
5. καλύπτω : I cover (up); hide, conceal (v. 24)	13. θαυμάζω : I wonder, marvel; admire (v. 27)
6. τὸ κῦμα : wave (v. 24)	14. ποταπός : how great, glorious? (v. 27)
7. καθεύδω : I sleep; am indifferent (v. 24)	15. ὑπακούω : I obey, follow (v. 27)
8. δειλός : cowardly, timid (v. 26)	

Matthew 8:21

- **αὐτοῦ** (The addition of αὐτοῦ is found in the majority of MSS [C L W Δ Θ 0250 *et al*], while it is missing in our oldest and most reliable MSS [א B as well as 33 it[a, (b, c, h, q)]]. It is most likely a scribal addition for the sake of clarification.)

22. **ἐπίτρεψόν**: Mood, mood usage? [1+2]

- **ἀπελθεῖν** (This is a complementary infinitive related to ἐπίτρεψον. It could be rendered, "[Permit me] to go" [cf. *Basics* 259–60; *ExSyn* 598–99].)

Matthew 8:22

23. ἀκολούθει: Mood, mood usage? [2+2]

_____

24. ἄφες: Mood, mood usage? [3+3]

_____

Matthew 8:23

- ἐμβάντι (This is a temporal participle of antecedent time related to ἠκολούθησαν. It could be rendered, "After he got into [the boat] ..." [cf. *Basics* 272-73; *ExSyn* 623-27]. This is also a rare instance of what might be called a dative absolute participle. It is the use of a dative adverbial participle at the front of a sentence with a noun or pronoun in the dative that is functioning as its subject; that noun/pronoun is then repeated in the dative case in the main clause. This is similar to the typical classical use of the genitive absolute [in which the genitive "subject" is repeated in the main clause in an oblique case].)

Matthew 8:24

- καλύπτεσθαι (This is an infinitive of result related to ὥστε. It could be rendered, "[a great storm came] so that [the ship] was covered ..." [cf. *Basics* 257-58; *ExSyn* 592-94]. It is also possible that *natural* result is intended by ὥστε plus the infinitive here. In classical Greek, ὥστε was used in dependent clauses to indicate natural or expected result when followed by an infinitive, actual result when followed by an indicative. There are only two instances of such a construction with an indicative in the NT [John 3:16; Gal 2:13], both of which probably follow the classical idiom.* Natural or expected result, in classical Greek, would have the force of "this is what we would expect to happen as a result of the main verb, but it might not happen" while actual result would mean, "this is what actually happens even though it might be unanticipated." Thus, in John 3:16 God loved the world *with the actual result* that he gave his Son—a result that would not necessarily be anticipated from the verb "loved" [ἠγάπησεν]. In Luke 5:7 we see an excellent illustration of natural/expected result with the infinitive: after Jesus told the disciples to cast their nets one more time after a night of catching nothing, they filled their boats so full of fish that the boats "began to sink" [βυθίζεσθαι]. Obviously, it wouldn't be a very helpful miracle if the boats ended up sinking from the miraculous catch of fish! Here, in Matt 8:24, the infinitive might also indicate natural or expected result *if* the idea of "cover" is that the waves so completely covered

---

* Contra BDF, who protest this usage, appealing to a poorly attested textual variant in John 3:16 and claiming that the construction with the indicative "is not genuine NT idiom" (BDF §391[2]).

the boat that it was submerged. If so, then καλύπτεσθαι should be translated with an ingressive force—"[the boat] began to get engulfed/swamped.")

Matthew 8:25

- **προσελθόντες** (This is an attendant circumstance participle related to ἤγειραν. Among the MSS, various clarifying words were added to this participle [οἱ μαθηταί, οἱ μαθηταὶ αὐτοῦ, and αὐτῷ οἱ μαθηταί]. These are all likely scribal additions since it was the tendency of scribes to clarify the text. The external evidence for the participle standing alone [א B 33[vid] it[a, aur, c]] also supports the shorter reading.)

- **σῶσον** (It should not come as a surprise, given the two textual variants already mentioned in this pericope, that some MSS have ἡμᾶς after σῶσον [L W Δ Θ 0242[vid]]. This is probably a scribal addition. The reading in the text has strong support [א B C f[1] f[13]]).

25. **σῶσον**: Mood, mood usage? [2+2]

_____

26. **ἀπολλύμεθα**: Voice, voice usage? [3+3]

_____

Matthew 8:26

- **ἐγερθείς** (This is an attendant circumstance participle related to ἐπετίμησεν.)

Lesson 13: Present Tense

Warm-Up Passages

Vocabulary

1. ἐπιγινώσκω : I know; perceive (Mk 2:8)	3. τοσοῦτος : so many (pl.); so much, so great (Jn 14:9)
2. διαλογίζομαι : I consider, ponder (Mk 2:8)	4. ὁ Φίλιππος : Philip (Jn 14:9)

Mark 2:8

καὶ εὐθὺς ἐπιγνοὺς ὁ Ἰησοῦς τῷ πνεύματι αὐτοῦ ὅτι οὕτως διαλογίζονται ἐν ἑαυτοῖς λέγει αὐτοῖς· τί ταῦτα διαλογίζεσθε ἐν ταῖς καρδίαις ὑμῶν;

1. **διαλογίζονται**: Tense, tense usage? [1+1]

   _____

2. **λέγει**: Tense, tense usage? [1+1]

   _____

3. **διαλογίζεσθε**: Tense, tense usage? [1+1]

   _____

John 14:9

λέγει αὐτῷ ὁ Ἰησοῦς· τοσούτῳ χρόνῳ μεθ' ὑμῶν εἰμι καὶ οὐκ ἔγνωκάς με, Φίλιππε;

4. **τοσούτῳ**: What definition does BDAG give this word? What is the basic difference between τοσοῦτος and τοιοῦτος? [2+2]

   _____

5. **εἰμι**: Tense, tense usage? [1+1]

   _____

● 1 John 4:8

ὁ θεὸς ἀγάπη ἐστίν.

6. **ἀγάπη**: This predicate nominative is in a particular kind of construction. See "Article, Part II" in either *Basics* or *ExSyn*. What is the name of the construction? What is most likely force of the anarthrous PN—indefinite, definite, or qualitative—and why (defend your answer in a sentence)? What exact kind of S-PN construction is this—convertible or subset? [1+1+2+2+2]

_____

_____

_____

7. **ἐστίν**: Tense, tense usage? [1+1]

_____

● Syntax Passages

Mark 14:32–42

Background

After Jesus' final Passover celebration with his disciples—the very meal which symbolized what Jesus was about to do as the suffering servant (14:12–26)—Jesus predicts that Peter will deny him thrice (14:27–31). Then, Jesus goes to the garden of Gethsemane and prays three times (14:32–42).

Text

14:32 Καὶ ἔρχονται εἰς χωρίον οὗ τὸ ὄνομα Γεθσημανὶ καὶ λέγει τοῖς μαθηταῖς αὐτοῦ· καθίσατε ὧδε ἕως προσεύξωμαι. **14:33** καὶ παραλαμβάνει τὸν Πέτρον καὶ τὸν Ἰάκωβον καὶ τὸν Ἰωάννην μετʼ αὐτοῦ καὶ ἤρξατο ἐκθαμβεῖσθαι καὶ ἀδημονεῖν **14:34** καὶ λέγει αὐτοῖς· περίλυπός ἐστιν ἡ ψυχή μου ἕως θανάτου· μείνατε ὧδε καὶ γρηγορεῖτε. **14:35** καὶ προελθὼν μικρὸν ἔπιπτεν ἐπὶ τῆς γῆς καὶ προσηύχετο ἵνα εἰ δυνατόν ἐστιν παρέλθῃ ἀπʼ αὐτοῦ ἡ ὥρα, **14:36** καὶ ἔλεγεν· ἀββα ὁ πατήρ, πάντα δυνατά σοι· παρένεγκε τὸ ποτήριον τοῦτο ἀπʼ ἐμοῦ· ἀλλʼ οὐ τί ἐγὼ θέλω ἀλλὰ τί σύ. **14:37** καὶ ἔρχεται καὶ εὑρίσκει αὐτοὺς καθεύδοντας, καὶ λέγει τῷ Πέτρῳ· Σίμων, καθεύδεις; οὐκ ἴσχυσας μίαν ὥραν γρηγορῆσαι; **14:38** γρηγορεῖτε καὶ προσεύχεσθε, ἵνα μὴ ἔλθητε εἰς πειρασμόν· τὸ μὲν πνεῦμα πρόθυμον ἡ δὲ σὰρξ ἀσθενής. **14:39** καὶ πάλιν ἀπελθὼν προσηύξατο τὸν αὐτὸν λόγον εἰπών. **14:40** καὶ πάλιν ἐλθὼν εὗρεν αὐτοὺς καθεύδοντας, ἦσαν γὰρ αὐτῶν οἱ ὀφθαλμοὶ καταβαρυνόμενοι, καὶ οὐκ ᾔδεισαν τί ἀποκριθῶσιν αὐτῷ. **14:41** καὶ ἔρχεται τὸ τρίτον καὶ λέγει αὐτοῖς· καθεύδετε τὸ λοιπὸν καὶ ἀναπαύεσθε· ἀπέχει· ἦλθεν ἡ ὥρα, ἰδοὺ παραδίδοται ὁ υἱὸς τοῦ ἀνθρώπου εἰς τὰς χεῖρας τῶν ἁμαρτωλῶν. **14:42** ἐγείρεσθε ἄγωμεν· ἰδοὺ ὁ παραδιδούς με ἤγγικεν.

Vocabulary

1. τὸ χωρίον : place, piece of land, field (v. 32)	14. ἀββα : father, abba (v. 36)
2. Γεθσημανί : Gethsemane (v. 32)	15. παραφέρω : I take or carry away, remove (v. 36)
3. καθίζω : I cause to sit down, sit (v. 32)	16. τὸ ποτήριον : cup, drinking vessel (v. 36)
4. παραλαμβάνω : I take, take along, receive (v. 33)	17. καθεύδω : I sleep; am indifferent (v. 37)
5. ὁ Ἰάκωβος : James (v. 33)	18. ἰσχύω : I am able (v. 37)
6. ἐκθαμβέω : I am very excited, overwhelmed (v. 33)	19. ὁ πειρασμός : test, trial, temptation (v. 38)
7. ἀδημονέω : I am distressed, troubled (v. 33)	20. πρόθυμος : ready, willing, eager (v. 38)
8. περίλυπος : very sad, deeply grieved (v. 34)	21. ἀσθενής : sick, ill; weak (v. 38)
9. γρηγορέω : I am watchful; I am on alert (v. 34)	22. καταβαρύνω : I weigh down; am heavy (pass. in NT) (v. 40)
10. προέρχομαι : I go forward, go before, proceed (v. 35)	23. ἀναπαύω : I cause to rest, give rest; rest (v. 41)
11. μικρός : small, short, little (v. 35)	24. ἀπέχω : I am paid in full, receive in full; it is enough (v. 41)
12. δυνατός : able, capable, powerful (v. 35)	25. ἁμαρτωλός : sinful; sinner (subst.) (v. 41)
13. παρέρχομαι : I go or pass by (v. 35)	26. ἐγγίζω : I draw near, approach (v. 42)

Mark 14:32

8. **ἕως**: What type of conjunction is this? [2]

_____

Mark 14:33

9. **παραλαμβάνει**: Tense, tense usage? [1+1]

_____

10. τὸν Πέτρον καὶ τὸν Ἰάκωβον καὶ τὸν Ἰωάννην: The second and third articles are lacking in some MSS. Assuming that they correctly reflect the original wording, this would constitute a TSKS construction or a Granville Sharp construction (see "Article, Part II" in *Basics* or *ExSyn*). Would it also fit the Granville Sharp rule? Defend your answer below. [2+2]

_____

_____

11. ἐκθαμβεῖσθαι: Tense, tense usage? (This is a complementary infinitive related to ἤρξατο. These infinitives help complete the thought of another verbal idea. It can be rendered, "[he began] to be alarmed/distressed" [cf. *Basics* 259-60; *ExSyn* 598-99].) [1+1]

_____

12. ἀδημονεῖν: Tense, tense usage? (This is a complementary infinitive related to ἤρξατο.) [1+1]

_____

Mark 14:34

13. ἐστιν: Tense, tense usage? [1+1]

_____

Mark 14:35

14. ἐστιν: Tense, tense usage? [1+1]

_____

Mark 14:36

15. παρένεγκε: Mood, use of mood? [1+1]

_____

16. θέλω: Tense, tense usage? [1+1]

_____

Mark 14:37

- **καθεύδοντας** (The accusative participle is related to the pronoun αὐτούς. It is possible that it is a complement in an object-complement construction and thus functioning adjectivally. This is possible because εὑρίσκω is the kind of verb that can take an object-complement double accusative. It could be temporal—"[he found them] as they were sleeping." Or it could be an indirect discourse participle. Such occur in the accusative case with a noun or pronoun in the accusative case after a verb or perception or communication [cf. *Basics* 281; *ExSyn* 645-46]. But whether εὑρίσκει qualifies as such a verb is problematic.)

17. **καθεύδοντας**: Tense, tense usage? [1+1]

_____

- **γρηγορῆσαι** (This is a complementary infinitive related to ἴσχυσας.)

Mark 14:38

18. **γρηγορεῖτε**: Tense, tense usage? [1+1]

_____

19. **προσεύχεσθε**: Tense, tense usage? [1+1]

_____

20. **μέν**: What type of conjunction is this? What conjunction is it balanced with? [1+1]

_____

Mark 14:39

- **ἀπελθών** (This is probably an attendant circumstance participle related to προσηύξατο. An attendant circumstance participle "is used to communicate an action that, in some sense, is coordinate with the finite verb" [*ExSyn* 640; cf. *Basics* 279; *ExSyn* 640-45]. Here it can be rendered, "He went away and [prayed the same thing].")

21. αὐτόν: What type of pronoun is this? What position is it in? How is it functioning? [1+1+1]

- εἰπών (This is a participle of means or redundant participle related to προσηύξατο. It can be rendered, "[he prayed] by saying" [cf. *Basics* 274-75; *ExSyn* 628-30].)

Mark 14:40

- ἐλθών (This is an attendant circumstance participle related to εὗρεν.)

22. καθεύδοντας: Tense, tense usage? (On the use of the participle, see the comment on καθεύδοντας in v. 37.) [1+1]

- καταβαρυνόμενοι (This is a periphrastic participle related to ἦσαν. A periphrastic participle is "a round-about way of saying what could be expressed by a single verb" [*ExSyn* 647; cf. *Basics* 281-82; *ExSyn* 647-49]. In combination with ἦσαν it is equivalent to an imperfect indicative.)

Mark 14:41

- ἀπέχει (Several MSS add τέλος, or omit ἀπέχει, to smooth out this reading. The reading in the text should remain since it is the harder reading and has ample external support [א A B C L Δ 083 f¹].)

23. ἀπέχει: Tense, tense usage? (Hint: look up this word in BDAG.) [1+1]

24. παραδίδοται: Tense, tense usage? The present tense for this indicative can be classified in at least three different ways. List two and explain briefly how the different uses can affect exegesis. [1+1+2+2]

Mark 14:42

25. ἐγείρεσθε: Tense, tense usage? [1+1]

_____

26. ἄγωμεν: Tense, tense usage? [1+1]

_____

27. παραδιδούς: What is the difference in meaning here between a futuristic present and a progressive present? Explain each briefly. [2+2]

_____

_____

Mark 2:16–18

Background

Confrontations with the Pharisees occur over Jesus' calling of Levi, a tax-collector, to be one of his disciples (2:13–17), and concerning regulations such as fasting (2:18–22) and the Sabbath (2:23–3:5).

Text

2:16 καὶ οἱ γραμματεῖς τῶν Φαρισαίων ἰδόντες ὅτι ἐσθίει μετὰ τῶν ἁμαρτωλῶν καὶ τελωνῶν ἔλεγον τοῖς μαθηταῖς αὐτοῦ· ὅτι μετὰ τῶν τελωνῶν καὶ ἁμαρτωλῶν ἐσθίει; **2:17** καὶ ἀκούσας ὁ Ἰησοῦς λέγει αὐτοῖς ὅτι οὐ χρείαν ἔχουσιν οἱ ἰσχύοντες ἰατροῦ ἀλλ' οἱ κακῶς ἔχοντες· οὐκ ἦλθον καλέσαι δικαίους ἀλλὰ ἁμαρτωλούς.

2:18 Καὶ ἦσαν οἱ μαθηταὶ Ἰωάννου καὶ οἱ Φαρισαῖοι νηστεύοντες. καὶ ἔρχονται καὶ λέγουσιν αὐτῷ· διὰ τί οἱ μαθηταὶ Ἰωάννου καὶ οἱ μαθηταὶ τῶν Φαρισαίων νηστεύουσιν, οἱ δὲ σοὶ μαθηταὶ οὐ νηστεύουσιν;

Vocabulary

1. ἁμαρτωλός : sinful, sinner (subst.) (v. 16)	5. ὁ ἰατρός : physician (v. 17)
2. ὁ τελώνης : tax collector, revenue officer (v. 16)	6. κακῶς : bad, badly, severely; with ἔχω, I am sick (v. 17)
3. ἡ χρεία : need, what should be (v. 17)	7. νηστεύω : I fast (v. 18)
4. ἰσχύω : I am in good health, healthy (v. 17)	8. σός : your (v. 18)

● Mark 2:16

- ἰδόντες (This is a temporal participle of antecedent time related to ἔλεγον. It can be rendered, "[after/when] they saw" [cf. *Basics* 272–73; *ExSyn* 623–27].)

28. τῶν ἁμαρτωλῶν καὶ τελωνῶν: What is this particular articular construction called? What is the relation between the two groups? Defend your answer briefly. [2+2+2]

_____

_____

29. ἐσθίει¹: Tense, tense usage? [1+2]

_____

- ἐσθίει² (There are several different variants found in the MS tradition that replace this word: [1] ἐσθίει καὶ πίνει [P⁸⁸ A f¹ 13 28 33 597 1505], (2) ἐσθίεται [Θ], (3) ἐσθίετε καὶ πίνετε [G Σ 565 700 1241] [4] ἐσθίει ὁ διδάσκαλος ὑμῶν [ℵ 1342 itᵃᵘʳ], [5] ἐσθίει καὶ πίνει ὁ διδάσκαλος ὑμῶν [L Δ f¹³ 1071], [6] ὁ διδάσκαλος ὑμῶν ἐσθίει καὶ πίνει [C 579]. The first and third readings are most likely scribal additions because of the assimilation to ἐσθίω and πίνω appearing side by side in other texts [cf. Matt 11:18, 19; Luke 5:30, 33; 7:34; 10:7]. The fourth and fifth readings are probably assimilations to Matt 9:11. The second reading seems to be a spelling variation from ἐσθίετε [the interchange between -ε and -αι was quite common among the MSS]. The reading in the text is most likely authentic since it has relatively strong external support [B D W 2427 itᵃ, ᵇ, ᵈ, ᵉ] and can best explain the rise of the other readings.)

30. ὅτι (This is not the conjunction ὅτι but the neuter singular of ὅστις. It is sometimes used in direct questions [as here] with the meaning "why?" The UBS⁴ gives a clue to help students know when the words to be translated are in a quotation: the first word of such sentences is capitalized. If a quotation is introduced by a recitative ὅτι, the word immediately following is capitalized. In this passage, the UBS⁴ capitalizes this word rather than the word following.) How is the capitalized ὅτι in the UBS text a clue that this is not the conjunction? [2]

_____

31. ἐσθίει²: There are at least three different possibilities for the use of the present tense. Name two and give an expanded gloss for each of them. [2+2]

_____

_____

Mark 2:17

- ἀκούσας (This is a temporal participle of antecedent time related to λέγει.)

32. ἔχουσιν: Tense, tense usage? [1+1]

_____

33. ἰσχύοντες: Tense, tense usage? [1+1]

_____

34. ἔχοντες: Tense, tense usage? [1+1]

_____

- καλέσαι (This is an infinitive of purpose related to ἦλθον. It can be rendered, "[I have not come] in order to call …" [cf. *Basics* 256-57; *ExSyn* 590-92].)

Mark 2:18

35. νηστεύοντες: Tense, tense usage? (This is a periphrastic participle related to ἦσαν.) [1+1]

_____

36. ἔρχονται: Tense, tense usage? [1+1]

_____

37. νηστεύουσιν[1]: Tense, tense usage? [1+1]

_____

38. νηστεύουσιν[2]: Tense, tense usage? [1+1]

_____

Lesson 14: Imperfect Tense

Warm-Up Passage

Vocabulary

1. ὁ γείτων : neighbor	3. ὁ προσαίτης : beggar
2. πρότερος : formerly, before	4. προσαιτέω : I beg

John 9:8

Οἱ οὖν γείτονες καὶ οἱ θεωροῦντες αὐτὸν τὸ πρότερον ὅτι προσαίτης ἦν ἔλεγον· οὐχ οὗτός ἐστιν ὁ καθήμενος καὶ προσαιτῶν;

1. ἦν: Tense, tense usage? [2+2]

_____

_____

Syntax Passages

John 5:16-19

Background

In Jesus' second visit to Jerusalem for "a feast of the Jews" (5:1) he gets involved in a Sabbath controversy (5:1-47). It is caused by his healing of a lame man (his third sign) by the pool of Bethesda (5:1-15). Because he performs such an act on the Sabbath, the Jews plot to kill him (5:16-18).

Text

5:16 καὶ διὰ τοῦτο ἐδίωκον οἱ Ἰουδαῖοι τὸν Ἰησοῦν, ὅτι ταῦτα ἐποίει ἐν σαββάτῳ.
5:17 Ὁ δὲ Ἰησοῦς ἀπεκρίνατο αὐτοῖς· ὁ πατήρ μου ἕως ἄρτι ἐργάζεται κἀγὼ ἐργάζομαι· **5:18** διὰ τοῦτο οὖν μᾶλλον ἐζήτουν αὐτὸν οἱ Ἰουδαῖοι ἀποκτεῖναι, ὅτι οὐ μόνον ἔλυεν τὸ σάββατον, ἀλλὰ καὶ πατέρα ἴδιον ἔλεγεν τὸν θεὸν ἴσον ἑαυτὸν ποιῶν τῷ θεῷ.
5:19 Ἀπεκρίνατο οὖν ὁ Ἰησοῦς καὶ ἔλεγεν αὐτοῖς· ἀμὴν ἀμὴν λέγω ὑμῖν, οὐ δύναται ὁ υἱὸς ποιεῖν ἀφ' ἑαυτοῦ οὐδὲν ἐὰν μή τι βλέπῃ τὸν πατέρα ποιοῦντα· ἃ γὰρ ἂν ἐκεῖνος ποιῇ, ταῦτα καὶ ὁ υἱὸς ὁμοίως ποιεῖ.

Vocabulary

1. διώκω : I persecute, pursue (v. 16)	4. λύω : I loose, untie, set free, destroy, abolish, allow (v. 18)
2. ἄρτι : now (v. 17)	5. ἴσος : equal, same, consistent (v. 18)
3. ἐργάζομαι : I work (v. 17)	6. ὁμοίως : likewise, so, similarly (v. 19)

John 5:16

2. **ἐδίωκον**: Give two possibilities for the imperfect with an appropriate translation for each. [3+3]

3. **ἐποίει**: Tense, tense usage? [2+2]

John 5:18

4. **πατέρα**: Case, case usage, word related to? [1+2+2]

5. **ἐζήτουν**: Tense, tense usage? [2+3]

6. **ἔλυεν**: Tense, tense usage? [2+2]

7. **ἔλεγεν**: Tense, tense usage? [2+2]

John 5:19

8. **ἔλεγεν**: Tense, tense usage? [2+2]

Acts 3:1–10

Background

The second major section of Acts deals with the expansion of the church in Jerusalem (3:1–6:7). This section opens with Peter healing a crippled man (3:1–10), an act that has repercussions (3:11–4:31).

Text

3:1 Πέτρος δὲ καὶ Ἰωάννης ἀνέβαινον εἰς τὸ ἱερὸν ἐπὶ τὴν ὥραν τῆς προσευχῆς τὴν ἐνάτην. **3:2** καί τις ἀνὴρ χωλὸς ἐκ κοιλίας μητρὸς αὐτοῦ ὑπάρχων ἐβαστάζετο, ὃν ἐτίθουν καθ᾽ ἡμέραν πρὸς τὴν θύραν τοῦ ἱεροῦ τὴν λεγομένην Ὡραίαν τοῦ αἰτεῖν ἐλεημοσύνην παρὰ τῶν εἰσπορευομένων εἰς τὸ ἱερόν· **3:3** ὃς ἰδὼν Πέτρον καὶ Ἰωάννην μέλλοντας εἰσιέναι εἰς τὸ ἱερόν, ἠρώτα ἐλεημοσύνην λαβεῖν. **3:4** ἀτενίσας δὲ Πέτρος εἰς αὐτὸν σὺν τῷ Ἰωάννῃ εἶπεν· βλέψον εἰς ἡμᾶς. **3:5** ὁ δὲ ἐπεῖχεν αὐτοῖς προσδοκῶν τι παρ᾽ αὐτῶν λαβεῖν. **3:6** εἶπεν δὲ Πέτρος· ἀργύριον καὶ χρυσίον οὐχ ὑπάρχει μοι, ὃ δὲ ἔχω τοῦτό σοι δίδωμι· ἐν τῷ ὀνόματι Ἰησοῦ Χριστοῦ τοῦ Ναζωραίου ἔγειρε καὶ περιπάτει. **3:7** καὶ πιάσας αὐτὸν τῆς δεξιᾶς χειρὸς ἤγειρεν αὐτόν· παραχρῆμα δὲ ἐστερεώθησαν αἱ βάσεις αὐτοῦ καὶ τὰ σφυδρά, **3:8** καὶ ἐξαλλόμενος ἔστη καὶ περιεπάτει καὶ εἰσῆλθεν σὺν αὐτοῖς εἰς τὸ ἱερὸν περιπατῶν καὶ ἁλλόμενος καὶ αἰνῶν τὸν θεόν. **3:9** καὶ εἶδεν πᾶς ὁ λαὸς αὐτὸν περιπατοῦντα καὶ αἰνοῦντα τὸν θεόν· **3:10** ἐπεγίνωσκον δὲ αὐτὸν ὅτι αὐτὸς ἦν ὁ πρὸς τὴν ἐλεημοσύνην καθήμενος ἐπὶ τῇ ὡραίᾳ πύλῃ τοῦ ἱεροῦ καὶ ἐπλήσθησαν θάμβους καὶ ἐκστάσεως ἐπὶ τῷ συμβεβηκότι αὐτῷ.

Vocabulary

1. ἡ προσευχή : prayer, intercession (v. 1)	16. ὁ Ναζωραῖος : Nazarene (v. 6)
2. ἔνατος : ninth (v. 1)	17. πιάζω : I grasp, take (hold of) (v. 7)
3. χωλός : lame, crippled (v. 2)	18. παραχρῆμα : at once, immediately (v. 7)
4. ἡ κοιλία : belly, stomach; womb (v. 2)	19. στερεόω : I make strong or firm (v. 7)
5. βαστάζω : I pick up, take up; carry (v. 2)	20. ἡ βάσις : foot (v. 7)
6. ἡ θύρα : door, gate, entrance (v. 2)	21. τὸ σφυδρόν : ankle (v. 7)
7. ὡραῖος : timely; beautiful (v. 2)	22. ἐξάλλομαι : I leap up (v. 8)
8. ἡ ἐλεημοσύνη : alms (giving) (v. 2)	23. ἅλλομαι : I leap, spring up (v. 8)

9. εἰσπορεύομαι : I go into, enter (v. 2)	24. αἰνέω : I praise (v. 8)
10. εἴσειμι : I go in or into (v. 3)	25. ἐπιγινώσκω : I know, understand, recognize, learn, notice (v. 10)
11. ἀτενίζω : I look intently at, stare (v. 4)	26. ἡ πύλη : gate, door (v. 10)
12. ἐπέχω : I hold fast; notice (v. 5)	27. πίμπλημι : I fill, fulfill (v. 10)
13. προσδοχάω : I wait for, expect (v. 5)	28. τὸ θάμβος : amazement, awe (v. 10)
14. τὸ ἀργύριον : silver money (v. 6)	29. ἡ ἔκστασις : amazement; ecstasy (v, 10)
15. τὸ χρυσίον : gold (v. 6)	30. συμβαίνω : I happen, come about (v. 10)

Acts 3:1

9. **ἀνέβαινον**: Tense, tense usage? [2+3]

_____

Acts 3:2

10. **ἐβαστάζετο**: Tense, tense usage? [2+2]

_____

11. **ἐτίθουν**: Tense, tense usage? Justify your answer briefly. [2+2+2]

_____

_____

12. **καθ᾽**: Look up the entry on κατά in BDAG and give the definition that is most appropriate for this context. [3]

_____

● Acts 3:3

13. ἠρώτα: Give an expanded translation for a progressive imperfect, an ingressive imperfect, and an iterative imperfect. Which one of these do you think this is? [2+2+2]

_____

_____

_____

Acts 3:4

14. βλέψον: Mood, mood usage? [2+3]

_____

● Acts 3:5

15. ἐπεῖχεν: Tense, tense usage? [2+2]

_____

Acts 3:6

16. χρυσίον: Case, case usage, word related to? [2+3+2]

_____

17. δίδωμι: Tense, tense usage? [2+2]

_____

Acts 3:8

18. περιεπάτει: Tense, tense usage? [2+2]

● _____

Acts 3:10

19. ἐπεγίνωσκον: Tense, tense usage? [2+2]

_____

20. ἦν: Tense, tense usage? [2+2]

_____

21. θάμβους: Case, case usage, word related to? [3+3+2]

_____

Lesson 15: Aorist and Future Tenses

Warm-Up Passages

Vocabulary

1. συσταυρόω : I crucify with (Ga 2:19)	5. ἀνέχω : I endure, bear with, put up with (mid. in NT) (Mk 9:19)
2. ὤ : O ... !; Oh, How ... ! (Mk 9:19)	7. κολοβόω : I shorten (Mk 13:20)
3. ἡ γενεά : race, kind; generation	8. ἐκλεκτός : chosen; elect; choice (Mk 13:20)
4. ἄπιστος : unbelievable, incredible; without faith, unbelieving (Mk 9:19)	9. ἐκλέγομαι : I choose, select, elect (Mk 13:20)
5. πότε : when? ἕως πότε means how long? (Mk 9:19)	

Galatians 2:19

ἐγὼ γὰρ διὰ νόμου νόμῳ ἀπέθανον, ἵνα θεῷ ζήσω. Χριστῷ συνεσταύρωμαι.

1. **νόμῳ**: Case, case usage, word related to? [1+1+1]

_____

2. **ἀπέθανον**: Tense, tense usage? [1+1]

_____

3. **ζήσω**: Tense, tense usage? [1+1]

_____

Mark 9:19

ὁ δὲ ἀποκριθεὶς αὐτοῖς λέγει· ὦ γενεὰ ἄπιστος, ἕως πότε πρὸς ὑμᾶς ἔσομαι; ἕως πότε ἀνέξομαι ὑμῶν; φέρετε αὐτὸν πρός με.

4. **ἀνέξομαι**: Tense, tense usage? [1+2]

_____

Mark 13:20

καὶ εἰ μὴ ἐκολόβωσεν κύριος τὰς ἡμέρας, οὐκ ἂν ἐσώθη πᾶσα σάρξ· ἀλλὰ διὰ τοὺς ἐκλεκτοὺς οὓς ἐξελέξατο ἐκολόβωσεν τὰς ἡμέρας.

5. **ἐσώθη**: Tense, tense usage? [1+2]

_____

6. **ἐκολόβωσεν**: Tense, tense usage? (Cf. the parallel in Matt 24:22 where the future tense is used.) [2+2]

_____

1 John 5:13

Ταῦτα ἔγραψα ὑμῖν ἵνα εἰδῆτε ὅτι ζωὴν ἔχετε αἰώνιον, τοῖς πιστεύουσιν εἰς τὸ ὄνομα τοῦ υἱοῦ τοῦ θεοῦ.

7. **ἔγραψα**: Tense, tense usage? [1+2]

_____

Syntax Passages

Luke 19:41–43

Background

Luke contrasts Jesus' positive ministry with the rising opposition to him. Jesus makes his so-called triumphal entry into Jerusalem (19:28–44) only to lament over the city's lack of awareness of what this presentation really meant (19:41–44).

Text

19:41 Καὶ ὡς ἤγγισεν ἰδὼν τὴν πόλιν ἔκλαυσεν ἐπ᾽ αὐτὴν **19:42** λέγων ὅτι εἰ ἔγνως ἐν τῇ ἡμέρᾳ ταύτῃ καὶ σὺ τὰ πρὸς εἰρήνην· νῦν δὲ ἐκρύβη ἀπὸ ὀφθαλμῶν σου. **19:43** ὅτι ἥξουσιν ἡμέραι ἐπὶ σὲ καὶ παρεμβαλοῦσιν οἱ ἐχθροί σου χάρακά σοι καὶ περικυκλώσουσίν σε καὶ συνέξουσίν σε πάντοθεν.

Vocabulary

1. ἐγγίζω : I approach, come near (v. 41)	6. ἐχθρός : hostile, hated, hating; enemy (subst.) (v. 43)
2. κλαίω : I weep, cry (v. 41)	7. ὁ χάραξ : palisade, entrenchment, siege-work (v. 43)
3. κρύπτω : I hide, keep secret (v. 42)	8. περικυκλόω : I surround, encircle
4. ἥκω : I have come, be present (v. 43)	9. συνέχω : I stop, shut; press hard; crowd (v. 43)
5. παρεμβάλλω : I put around, surround (v. 43)	10. πάντοθεν : from all directions, on all sides, entirely (v. 43)

Luke 19:41

8. ἤγγισεν: Tense, tense usage? [1+2]

_____

9. ἰδών: Tense, tense usage? [1+1]

_____

10. ἔκλαυσεν: Tense, tense usage? [1+1]

_____

Luke 19:42

11. ἔγνως: Mood, mood usage? [1+2]

_____

12. ἔγνως: Tense, tense usage? [2+2]

_____

13. τά: Structural category? [3]

_____

14. ἐκρύβη: Tense, tense usage? [1+2]

_____

Luke 19:43

15. ἥξουσιν: Tense, tense usage? [1+2]

_____

16. παρεμβαλοῦσιν: Tense, tense usage? [1+1]

_____

17. περικυκλώσουσιν: Tense, tense usage? [1+1]

_____

18. *συνέξουσιν*: Tense, tense usage? [1+1]

_____

Matthew 21:17-21

Background

Jesus presented himself formally with his triumphal entry into Jerusalem (21:1-11). It is evident that although the religious leaders did not accept him (21:15), many of the populace did (21:16-17). Even though Jesus was the Messiah, he was rejected by Israel (21:18-22:46). The nation simply failed to accept him as king, Messiah, and Son of Man—as he defined the terms. This segment begins with a foreshadowing of the nation's rejection by God in that a fig tree was cursed and withered because it did not bear fruit (21:18-22).

Text

21:17 Καὶ καταλιπὼν αὐτοὺς ἐξῆλθεν ἔξω τῆς πόλεως εἰς Βηθανίαν καὶ ηὐλίσθη ἐκεῖ.
21:18 Πρωῒ δὲ ἐπανάγων εἰς τὴν πόλιν ἐπείνασεν. **21:19** καὶ ἰδὼν συκῆν μίαν ἐπὶ τῆς ὁδοῦ ἦλθεν ἐπ' αὐτὴν καὶ οὐδὲν εὗρεν ἐν αὐτῇ εἰ μὴ φύλλα μόνον, καὶ λέγει αὐτῇ· μηκέτι ἐκ σοῦ καρπὸς γένηται εἰς τὸν αἰῶνα. καὶ ἐξηράνθη παραχρῆμα ἡ συκῆ.
21:20 Καὶ ἰδόντες οἱ μαθηταὶ ἐθαύμασαν λέγοντες· πῶς παραχρῆμα ἐξηράνθη ἡ συκῆ; **21:21** ἀποκριθεὶς δὲ ὁ Ἰησοῦς εἶπεν αὐτοῖς· ἀμὴν λέγω ὑμῖν, ἐὰν ἔχητε πίστιν καὶ μὴ διακριθῆτε, οὐ μόνον τὸ τῆς συκῆς ποιήσετε, ἀλλὰ κἂν τῷ ὄρει τούτῳ εἴπητε· ἄρθητι καὶ βλήθητι εἰς τὴν θάλασσαν, γενήσεται.

Vocabulary

1. καταλείπω : I leave (behind); leave (v. 17)	8. τὸ φύλλον : leaf; foliage (pl. in NT) (v. 19)
2. ἡ Βηθανία : Bethany (v. 17)	9. μηκέτι : no longer (v. 19)
3. αὐλίζομαι : I spend the night (v. 17)	10. ξηραίνω : I wither, become dry, dry up (v. 19)
4. πρωΐ : early, early in the morning (v. 18)	11. παραχρῆμα : at once, immediately (v. 19)
5. ἐπανάγω : I return; go out, push off (v. 18)	12. θαυμάζω : I wonder, marvel; admire (v. 20)
6. πεινάω : I hunger, am hungry (v. 18)	13. διακρίνω : I doubt; make a distinction, differentiate, distinguish (v. 21)
7. ἡ συχῆ : fig tree (v. 19)	14. κἄν : and if, whether; even if, at least (v. 21)

Matthew 21:17

19. **καταλιπών**: Tense, tense usage? [1+2]

_____

20. **ἐξῆλθεν**: Tense, tense usage? [1+1]

_____

21. **ηὐλίσθη**: Tense, tense usage? [1+1]

_____

Matthew 21:18

22. **ἐπείνασεν**: Tense, tense usage? [1+2]

_____

_____

Matthew 21:19

23. ἰδών: Tense, tense usage? [1+1]

_____

24. ἦλθεν: Tense, tense usage? [1+1]

_____

25. εὗρεν: Tense, tense usage? [1+1]

_____

26. γένηται: Tense, tense usage? [1+2]

_____

27. ἐξηράνθη: Tense, tense usage? [1+1]

_____

28. ἐξηράνθη: Compare this to Mark 11:11–14, 20 (read the text in English). When does the fig tree wither in Mark? How do you explain these differences? [3+3]

_____

_____

Matthew 21:20

29. ἰδόντες: Tense, tense usage? [1+1]

_____

30. ἐθαύμασαν: Tense, tense usage? [1+1]

_____

31. ἐξηράνθη: Tense, tense usage? [1+1]

_____

● Matthew 21:21

32. ἀποκριθείς: Tense, tense usage? [1+1]

_____

33. εἶπεν: Tense, tense usage? [1+1]

_____

34. ἔχητε: Tense, tense usage? [2+2]

_____

35. διακριθῆτε: Tense, tense usage? [1+2]

_____

36. ποιήσετε: Tense, tense usage? [1+2]

_____

37. εἴπητε: Tense, tense usage? [1+1]

_____

38. γενήσεται: Tense, tense usage? [1+1]

_____

Lesson 16: Perfect and Pluperfect Tenses

Syntax Passage

John 11:11-44

Background

In this final confrontation with the religious leaders, Jesus raises a man from the dead (the last of seven "signs: in John) (10:40-11:44). The result is that many Jews believe in him (11:45), but the religious leaders seek his death (11:46-57).

Text

11:11 Ταῦτα εἶπεν, καὶ μετὰ τοῦτο λέγει αὐτοῖς· Λάζαρος ὁ φίλος ἡμῶν κεκοίμηται· ἀλλὰ πορεύομαι ἵνα ἐξυπνίσω αὐτόν. **11:12** εἶπαν οὖν οἱ μαθηταὶ αὐτῷ· κύριε, εἰ κεκοίμηται σωθήσεται. **11:13** εἰρήκει δὲ ὁ Ἰησοῦς περὶ τοῦ θανάτου αὐτοῦ, ἐκεῖνοι δὲ ἔδοξαν ὅτι περὶ τῆς κοιμήσεως τοῦ ὕπνου λέγει. **11:14** τότε οὖν εἶπεν αὐτοῖς ὁ Ἰησοῦς παρρησίᾳ· Λάζαρος ἀπέθανεν, **11:15** καὶ χαίρω δι᾽ ὑμᾶς ἵνα πιστεύσητε, ὅτι οὐκ ἤμην ἐκεῖ· ἀλλὰ ἄγωμεν πρὸς αὐτόν. **11:16** εἶπεν οὖν Θωμᾶς ὁ λεγόμενος Δίδυμος τοῖς συμμαθηταῖς· ἄγωμεν καὶ ἡμεῖς ἵνα ἀποθάνωμεν μετ᾽ αὐτοῦ.

11:17 Ἐλθὼν οὖν ὁ Ἰησοῦς εὗρεν αὐτὸν τέσσαρας ἤδη ἡμέρας ἔχοντα ἐν τῷ μνημείῳ. **11:18** ἦν δὲ ἡ Βηθανία ἐγγὺς τῶν Ἱεροσολύμων ὡς ἀπὸ σταδίων δεκαπέντε. **11:19** πολλοὶ δὲ ἐκ τῶν Ἰουδαίων ἐληλύθεισαν πρὸς τὴν Μάρθαν καὶ Μαριὰμ ἵνα παραμυθήσωνται αὐτὰς περὶ τοῦ ἀδελφοῦ. **11:20** ἡ οὖν Μάρθα ὡς ἤκουσεν ὅτι Ἰησοῦς ἔρχεται ὑπήντησεν αὐτῷ· Μαριὰμ δὲ ἐν τῷ οἴκῳ ἐκαθέζετο. **11:21** εἶπεν οὖν ἡ Μάρθα πρὸς τὸν Ἰησοῦν· κύριε, εἰ ἦς ὧδε οὐκ ἂν ἀπέθανεν ὁ ἀδελφός μου· **11:22** ἀλλὰ καὶ νῦν οἶδα ὅτι ὅσα ἂν αἰτήσῃ τὸν θεὸν δώσει σοι ὁ θεός. **11:23** λέγει αὐτῇ ὁ Ἰησοῦς· ἀναστήσεται ὁ ἀδελφός σου. **11:24** λέγει αὐτῷ ἡ Μάρθα· οἶδα ὅτι ἀναστήσεται ἐν τῇ ἀναστάσει ἐν τῇ ἐσχάτῃ ἡμέρᾳ. **11:25** εἶπεν αὐτῇ ὁ Ἰησοῦς· ἐγώ εἰμι ἡ ἀνάστασις καὶ ἡ ζωή· ὁ πιστεύων εἰς ἐμὲ κἂν ἀποθάνῃ ζήσεται, **11:26** καὶ πᾶς ὁ ζῶν καὶ πιστεύων εἰς ἐμὲ οὐ μὴ ἀποθάνῃ εἰς τὸν αἰῶνα. πιστεύεις τοῦτο; **11:27** λέγει αὐτῷ· ναὶ κύριε, ἐγὼ πεπίστευκα ὅτι σὺ εἶ ὁ χριστὸς ὁ υἱὸς τοῦ θεοῦ ὁ εἰς τὸν κόσμον ἐρχόμενος.

11:28 Καὶ τοῦτο εἰποῦσα ἀπῆλθεν καὶ ἐφώνησεν Μαριὰμ τὴν ἀδελφὴν αὐτῆς λάθρα εἰποῦσα· ὁ διδάσκαλος πάρεστιν καὶ φωνεῖ σε. **11:29** ἐκείνη δὲ ὡς ἤκουσεν ἠγέρθη ταχὺ καὶ ἤρχετο πρὸς αὐτόν. **11:30** οὔπω δὲ ἐληλύθει ὁ Ἰησοῦς εἰς τὴν κώμην, ἀλλ᾽ ἦν ἔτι ἐν τῷ τόπῳ ὅπου ὑπήντησεν αὐτῷ ἡ Μάρθα. **11:31** οἱ οὖν Ἰουδαῖοι οἱ ὄντες μετ᾽ αὐτῆς ἐν τῇ οἰκίᾳ καὶ παραμυθούμενοι αὐτήν, ἰδόντες τὴν Μαριὰμ ὅτι ταχέως ἀνέστη καὶ ἐξῆλθεν, ἠκολούθησαν αὐτῇ δόξαντες ὅτι ὑπάγει εἰς τὸ μνημεῖον ἵνα κλαύσῃ ἐκεῖ.

11:32 Ἡ οὖν Μαριὰμ ὡς ἦλθεν ὅπου ἦν Ἰησοῦς ἰδοῦσα αὐτὸν ἔπεσεν αὐτοῦ πρὸς τοὺς πόδας λέγουσα αὐτῷ· κύριε, εἰ ἦς ὧδε οὐκ ἄν μου ἀπέθανεν ὁ ἀδελφός. **11:33** Ἰησοῦς οὖν ὡς εἶδεν αὐτὴν κλαίουσαν καὶ τοὺς συνελθόντας αὐτῇ Ἰουδαίους κλαίοντας, ἐνεβριμήσατο τῷ πνεύματι καὶ ἐτάραξεν ἑαυτὸν **11:34** καὶ εἶπεν· ποῦ τεθείκατε αὐτόν; λέγουσιν αὐτῷ· κύριε, ἔρχου καὶ ἴδε. **11:35** ἐδάκρυσεν ὁ Ἰησοῦς. **11:36** ἔλεγον οὖν οἱ Ἰουδαῖοι· ἴδε πῶς ἐφίλει αὐτόν. **11:37** τινὲς δὲ ἐξ αὐτῶν εἶπαν· οὐκ ἐδύνατο οὗτος ὁ ἀνοίξας τοὺς ὀφθαλμοὺς τοῦ τυφλοῦ ποιῆσαι ἵνα καὶ οὗτος μὴ ἀποθάνῃ;

150

11:38 Ἰησοῦς οὖν πάλιν ἐμβριμώμενος ἐν ἑαυτῷ ἔρχεται εἰς τὸ μνημεῖον· ἦν δὲ σπήλαιον καὶ λίθος ἐπέκειτο ἐπ᾽ αὐτῷ. **11:39** λέγει ὁ Ἰησοῦς· ἄρατε τὸν λίθον. λέγει αὐτῷ ἡ ἀδελφὴ τοῦ τετελευτηκότος Μάρθα· κύριε, ἤδη ὄζει, τεταρταῖος γάρ ἐστιν. **11:40** λέγει αὐτῇ ὁ Ἰησοῦς· οὐκ εἶπόν σοι ὅτι ἐὰν πιστεύσῃς ὄψῃ τὴν δόξαν τοῦ θεοῦ; **11:41** ἦραν οὖν τὸν λίθον. ὁ δὲ Ἰησοῦς ἦρεν τοὺς ὀφθαλμοὺς ἄνω καὶ εἶπεν· πάτερ, εὐχαριστῶ σοι ὅτι ἤκουσάς μου. **11:42** ἐγὼ δὲ ᾔδειν ὅτι πάντοτέ μου ἀκούεις, ἀλλὰ διὰ τὸν ὄχλον τὸν περιεστῶτα εἶπον, ἵνα πιστεύσωσιν ὅτι σύ με ἀπέστειλας. **11:43** καὶ ταῦτα εἰπὼν φωνῇ μεγάλῃ ἐκραύγασεν· Λάζαρε, δεῦρο ἔξω. **11:44** ἐξῆλθεν ὁ τεθνηκὼς δεδεμένος τοὺς πόδας καὶ τὰς χεῖρας κειρίαις καὶ ἡ ὄψις αὐτοῦ σουδαρίῳ περιεδέδετο. λέγει αὐτοῖς ὁ Ἰησοῦς· λύσατε αὐτὸν καὶ ἄφετε αὐτὸν ὑπάγειν.

Vocabulary

1. ὁ Λάζαρος : Lazarus (v. 11)	30. οὔπω : not yet (v. 30)
2. φίλος : beloved; friend (subst.) (v. 11)	31. ἡ κώμη : village, small town (v. 30)
3. κοιμάω : I sleep; die (v. 11)	32. ταχέως : quickly, without delay (v. 31)
4. ἐξυπνίζω : I wake up, arouse (v. 11)	33. κλαίω : I weep, cry (v. 31)
5. ἡ κοίμησις : sleep (v. 13)	34. συνέρχομαι : I assemble; travel together with (v. 33)
6. ὁ ὕπνος : sleep (fig. and lit.) (v. 13)	35. ἐμβριμάομαι : I warn sternly, scold; am deeply moved (v. 33)
7. ἡ παρρησία : outspokenness; confidence, courage (v. 14)	36. ταράσσω : I stir up; disturb (v. 33)
8. ὁ Θωμᾶς : Thomas (v. 16)	37. πόν : where? (v. 34)
9. ὁ Δίδυμος : Didymus (v. 16)	38. ἴδε : look, see, behold (v. 36)
10. ὁ συμμαθητής : fellow-disciple (v. 16)	39. δακρύω : I weep (v. 35)
11. τέσσαρες : four (v. 17)	40. φιλέω : I love (v. 36)
12. τὸ μνημεῖον : monument; grave (v. 17)	41. τὸ σπήλαιον : cave, hideout (v. 38)
13. ἡ Βηθανία : Bethany (v. 18)	42. ἐπίκειμαι : I lie upon or on (v. 38)
14. ἐγγύς : near, close to (v. 18)	43. τελευτάω : I die (v. 39)
15. τὸ στάδιον : stade; arena, stadium (v. 18)	44. ὄζω : I emit an odor, smell, stink (v. 39)
16. δεκαπέντε : fifteen (v. 18)	45. τεταρταῖος : happening on the fourth day (v. 39)
17. ἡ Μάρθα : Martha (v. 19)	46. ἄνω : above; upward; heaven (v. 41)
18. ἡ Μαρίαμ : Mary (v. 19)	47. εὐχαριστέω : I am thankful (v. 41)

19. παραμυθέομαι : I cheer up, console, comfort (v. 19)	48. πάντοτε : always, at all times (v. 42)
20. ὑπαντάω : I meet (v. 20)	49. περιΐστημι : I stand around; avoid, shun (mid.) (v. 42)
21. καθέζομαι : I sit, remain (v. 20)	50. κραυγάζω : I cry out, scream (v. 43)
22. ἡ ἀνάστασις : rising up; resurrection (v. 24)	51. δεῦρο : come here (v. 43)
23. κἄν : and if; whether; even though (v. 25)	52. θνῄσκω : I die (v. 44)
24. ναί : yes (v. 27)	53. δέω : I bind, tie (v. 44)
25. φωνέω : I call or cry out, speak loudly (v. 28)	54. ἡ κειρία : binding material (v. 44)
26. ἡ ἀδελφή : sister, fellow believer (v. 28)	55. ἡ ὄψις : outward appearance; face (v. 44)
27. λάθρα : secretly (v. 28)	56. τὸ σουδάριον : face-cloth, cloth (v. 44)
28. πάρειμι : I am present, have come (v. 28)	57. περιδέω : I bind or wrap around (v. 44)
29. ταχύς : quick, swift (v. 29)	58. λύω : I loose; untie; break up (v. 44)

John 11:11

1. **κεκοίμηται**: Tense, tense usage? [1+2]

_____

John 11:12

2. **κεκοίμηται**: Tense, tense usage? [1+1]

_____

John 11:13

3. **εἰρήκει**: Tense, tense usage? [2+2]

_____

●   4. λέγει: Tense, use of tense? [1+2]

_____

John 11:15

   5. ὅτι: Use of ὅτι clause, word related to? [2+2]

_____

   6. ἄγωμεν: Mood, use of mood? [2+2]

_____

John 11:17

   7. ἡμέρας: Case, case usage, word related to? [1+1+1]

●

_____

John 11:19

   8. ἐληλύθεισαν: Tense, tense usage? [2+2]

_____

   9. τὴν Μάρθαν καὶ Μαριάμ: What kind of articular construction is this? What are the semantics involved? [2+1]

_____

John 11:22

   10. οἶδα: Tense, tense usage? [1+1]

_____

●   11. αἰτήσῃ: Mood, use of mood? [1+2]

_____

John 11:24

12. οἶδα: Tense, tense usage? [1+1]

_____

John 11:26

13. πᾶς ὁ ζῶν καὶ πιστεύων: What kind of articular construction is this (see "Article, Part II" in either *Basics* or *ExSyn*). Does it fit the rule? [2+2]

_____

John 11:27

14. πεπίστευκα: Tense, tense usage? [1+2]

_____

John 11:29

15. ἤρχετο: Tense, use of tense? [2+2]

_____

John 11:30

16. οὔπω: What type of conjunction is this? [2]

_____

17. ἐληλύθει: Tense, tense usage? [2+2]

_____

John 11:34

18. τεθείκατε: Tense, tense usage? [2+2]

_____

19. ἔρχου: Mood, use of mood? [2+2]

_____

John 11:36

20. ἐφίλει: Tense, tense usage? [2+2]

_____

John 11:37

21. ἵνα: Use of the ἵνα clause, word related to? [2+2]

_____

John 11:38

22. ἐπέκειτο: Tense, tense usage? [2+2]

_____

John 11:39

23. τετελευτηκότος: Tense, tense usage? [1+2]

_____

24. ἐστιν: Tense, tense usage? [1+2]

_____

John 11:42

25. ἤδειν: Tense, tense usage? [2+2]

_____

26. περιεστῶτα: Tense, tense usage? [2+2]

_____

John 11:43

27. Λάζαρε: Case, case usage? [1+1]

_____

John 11:44

28. τεθνηκώς: Tense, tense usage? [1+2]

_____

29. δεδεμένος: Tense, tense usage? [1+2]

_____

30. περιεδέδετο: Tense, tense usage? [2+2]

_____

Lesson 17: Infinitive

Warm-Up Passages

Vocabulary

1. περισσεύω : I abound, overflow, excel (Ro 15:13)	5. παραγίνομαι : I arrive, come, draw near (Mt 3:13)
2. παύω : I stop, I cease (1 Pt 3:10)	6. ἀνάγω : I lead, bring up (Mt 4:1)
3. τὸ χεῖλος : lips (pl.) (1 Pt 3:10)	7. ἔρημος : desert, wilderness (subst.) (Mt 4:1)
4. ὁ δόλος : deceit, cunning (1 Pt 3:10)	8. πειράζω : I put to the test, tempt (Mt 4:1)

Romans 15:13

ὁ δὲ θεὸς τῆς ἐλπίδος πληρώσαι ὑμᾶς πάσης χαρᾶς καὶ εἰρήνης ἐν τῷ πιστεύειν, εἰς τὸ περισσεύειν ὑμᾶς ἐν τῇ ἐλπίδι ἐν δυνάμει πνεύματος ἁγίου.

- **πληρώσαι** (Although this form may look like an infinitive, it is actually an optative. It is a voluntative optative expressing a wish: "May the God of hope fill you…." The difference is the accent: the aorist optative form for this verb is πληρώσαι while the aorist infinitive is πληρῶσαι.)

1. **πιστεύειν**: Infinitive structure, infinitive usage, word related to? [1+1+1]

   _____

2. **περισσεύειν**: Infinitive structure, infinitive usage, word related to? [1+1+1]

   _____

   _____

John 8:58

εἶπεν αὐτοῖς Ἰησοῦς· ἀμὴν ἀμὴν λέγω ὑμῖν, πρὶν Ἀβραὰμ γενέσθαι ἐγὼ εἰμί.

3. **γενέσθαι**: Infinitive structure, infinitive usage, word related to? [1+1+1]

   _____

Mark 1:14

Μετὰ δὲ τὸ παραδοθῆναι τὸν Ἰωάννην ἦλθεν ὁ Ἰησοῦς εἰς τὴν Γαλιλαίαν κηρύσσων τὸ εὐαγγέλιον τοῦ θεοῦ.

4. **παραδοθῆναι**: Infinitive structure, infinitive usage, word related to? [1+1+1]

_____

1 Peter 3:10

> ὁ γὰρ θέλων ζωὴν ἀγαπᾶν
> 　　καὶ ἰδεῖν ἡμέρας ἀγαθὰς
> παυσάτω τὴν γλῶσσαν ἀπὸ κακοῦ
> 　　καὶ χείλη τοῦ μὴ λαλῆσαι δόλον.

5. **ἀγαπᾶν**: Infinitive structure, infinitive usage, word related to? [1+1+1]

_____

6. **ἰδεῖν**: Infinitive structure, infinitive usage, word related to? [1+1+1]

_____

7. **λαλῆσαι**: Infinitive structure, infinitive usage, word related to? (This use of the infinitive is not classified either in *Basics* or *ExSyn*. If you treat it as a substantive, however, you might be able to figure it out.) [1+1+1]

_____

Matt 3:13

Τότε παραγίνεται ὁ Ἰησοῦς ἀπὸ τῆς Γαλιλαίας ἐπὶ τὸν Ἰορδάνην πρὸς τὸν Ἰωάννην τοῦ βαπτισθῆναι ὑπ᾽ αὐτοῦ.

8. **βαπτισθῆναι**: Infinitive structure, infinitive usage, word related to? [1+1+1]

_____

Matt 4:1

Τότε ὁ Ἰησοῦς ἀνήχθη εἰς τὴν ἔρημον ὑπὸ τοῦ πνεύματος πειρασθῆναι ὑπὸ τοῦ διαβόλου.

9. πειρασθῆναι: Infinitive structure, infinitive usage, word related to? [1+1+1]

Syntax Passages

Mark 4:1-6

Background

In chapter 4 Mark treats us to his second longest section of didactic material (chapter 13, the Olivet Discourse, being the longest). The parables were given in a context of both hostility (from the religious leaders) and enormous popularity (from the crowd). The first group of parables deals with the responsibility of the hearers (4:3-25). This includes two parables, as well as an aside to the disciples about the purpose of the parables. In the parable of the sower, Jesus argues that his hearers are like seed that is sown; they are to grow and be productive (4:3-9; 4:13-20), though not all who hear will really listen and heed (4:10-12).

Text

4:1 Καὶ πάλιν ἤρξατο διδάσκειν παρὰ τὴν θάλασσαν· καὶ συνάγεται πρὸς αὐτὸν ὄχλος πλεῖστος, ὥστε αὐτὸν εἰς πλοῖον ἐμβάντα καθῆσθαι ἐν τῇ θαλάσσῃ, καὶ πᾶς ὁ ὄχλος πρὸς τὴν θάλασσαν ἐπὶ τῆς γῆς ἦσαν. **4:2** καὶ ἐδίδασκεν αὐτοὺς ἐν παραβολαῖς πολλὰ καὶ ἔλεγεν αὐτοῖς ἐν τῇ διδαχῇ αὐτοῦ·

4:3 Ἀκούετε. ἰδοὺ ἐξῆλθεν ὁ σπείρων σπεῖραι. **4:4** καὶ ἐγένετο ἐν τῷ σπείρειν ὃ μὲν ἔπεσεν παρὰ τὴν ὁδόν, καὶ ἦλθεν τὰ πετεινὰ καὶ κατέφαγεν αὐτό. **4:5** καὶ ἄλλο ἔπεσεν ἐπὶ τὸ πετρῶδες ὅπου οὐκ εἶχεν γῆν πολλήν, καὶ εὐθὺς ἐξανέτειλεν διὰ τὸ μὴ ἔχειν βάθος γῆς· **4:6** καὶ ὅτε ἀνέτειλεν ὁ ἥλιος ἐκαυματίσθη καὶ διὰ τὸ μὴ ἔχειν ῥίζαν ἐξηράνθη.

Vocabulary

1. πλεῖστος : superl. of πολύς; very great, as elative (v. 1)	8. τὸ βάθος : depth, deep water (v. 5)
2. ἐμβαίνω : I step or get into, embark (v. 1)	9. ἀνατέλλω : I rise, cause to rise (v. 6)
3. ἡ διδαχή : instruction (act); teaching (content) (v. 2)	10. ὁ ἥλιος : sun (v. 6)
4. τὸ πετεινόν : bird (v. 4)	11. καυματίζω : I burn up, scorch (v. 6)
5. κατεσθίω : I eat up, consume (v. 4)	12. ἡ ῥίζα : root; descendant (v. 6)
6. πετρώδης : rocky, stony (v. 5)	13. ξηραίνω : I dry (up); wither (v. 6)
7. ἐξανατέλλω : I spring up (v. 5)	

Mark 4:1

10. διδάσκειν: Infinitive structure, infinitive usage, word related to? [1+1+1]

_____

11. πλεῖστος: Adjective position, use of form? [1+1]

_____

12. καθῆσθαι: Infinitive structure, infinitive usage, word related to? [1+1+1]

_____

Mark 4:2

13. ἐδίδασκεν: Tense, tense usage? [1+1]

_____

Mark 4:3

14. ὁ: Semantic category of the article? [2]

_____

15. σπεῖραι: Infinitive structure, infinitive usage, word related to? [1+1+1]

_____

Mark 4:4

16. σπείρειν: Infinitive structure, infinitive usage, word related to? [1+1+1]

_____

17. αὐτό: What is the antecedent of this pronoun? [3]

_____

●Mark 4:5

18. ἔχειν: Infinitive structure, infinitive usage, word related to? [1+1+1]

_____

Mark 4:6

19. ἔχειν: Infinitive structure, infinitive usage, word related to? [1+1+1]

_____

1 Thessalonians 4:1–9

Background

Paul here argues that the manner of the believers' lifestyle should be characterized by proper relations within the body (4:1-12). In 4:1-2 he summarizes this by stating that the Thessalonians' lifestyle should be characterized by continually pleasing God (4:1-2). Then he gives specifics (4:3-12): (1) negatively, a believer's lifestyle should be characterized by the absence of irresponsible lust (4:3-8); (2) positively, a believer's lifestyle should be characterized by a mutual edification (extending beyond the local body) and an individual work ethic (affecting the unbeliever's view of the church) (4:9-12).

Text

4:1 Λοιπὸν οὖν, ἀδελφοί, ἐρωτῶμεν ὑμᾶς καὶ παρακαλοῦμεν ἐν κυρίῳ Ἰησοῦ, ἵνα καθὼς παρελάβετε παρ᾽ ἡμῶν τὸ πῶς δεῖ ὑμᾶς περιπατεῖν καὶ ἀρέσκειν θεῷ, καθὼς καὶ περιπατεῖτε, ἵνα περισσεύητε μᾶλλον. **4:2** οἴδατε γὰρ τίνας παραγγελίας ἐδώκαμεν ὑμῖν διὰ τοῦ κυρίου Ἰησοῦ.

4:3 Τοῦτο γάρ ἐστιν θέλημα τοῦ θεοῦ, ὁ ἁγιασμὸς ὑμῶν, ἀπέχεσθαι ὑμᾶς ἀπὸ τῆς πορνείας, **4:4** εἰδέναι ἕκαστον ὑμῶν τὸ ἑαυτοῦ σκεῦος κτᾶσθαι ἐν ἁγιασμῷ καὶ τιμῇ, **4:5** μὴ ἐν πάθει ἐπιθυμίας καθάπερ καὶ τὰ ἔθνη τὰ μὴ εἰδότα τὸν θεόν, **4:6** τὸ μὴ ὑπερβαίνειν καὶ πλεονεκτεῖν ἐν τῷ πράγματι τὸν ἀδελφὸν αὐτοῦ, διότι ἔκδικος κύριος περὶ πάντων τούτων, καθὼς καὶ προείπαμεν ὑμῖν καὶ διεμαρτυράμεθα. **4:7** οὐ γὰρ ἐκάλεσεν ἡμᾶς ὁ θεὸς ἐπὶ ἀκαθαρσίᾳ ἀλλ᾽ ἐν ἁγιασμῷ. **4:8** τοιγαροῦν ὁ ἀθετῶν οὐκ ἄνθρωπον ἀθετεῖ ἀλλὰ τὸν θεὸν τὸν καὶ διδόντα τὸ πνεῦμα αὐτοῦ τὸ ἅγιον εἰς ὑμᾶς.

4:9 Περὶ δὲ τῆς φιλαδελφίας οὐ χρείαν ἔχετε γράφειν ὑμῖν, αὐτοὶ γὰρ ὑμεῖς θεοδίδακτοί ἐστε εἰς τὸ ἀγαπᾶν ἀλλήλους,

Vocabulary

1. παραλαμβάνω : I receive; take, bring along (v. 1)	14. ὑπερβαίνω : I trespass, sin (v. 6)
2. ἀρέσκω : I win favor; please (v. 1)	15. πλεονεκτέω : I exploit, outwit, cheat (v. 6)
3. περισσεύω : I abound, surpass (v. 1)	16. τὸ πρᾶγμα : event, occurrence, matter (v. 6)
4. ἡ παραγγελία : order, command (v. 2)	17. διότι : because; therefore, for (v. 6)
5. ὁ ἁγιασμός : holiness, sanctification (v. 3)	18. ἔκδικος : punishing; one who punishes (as subst.) (v. 6)
6. ἀπέχω : abstain, refrain from (v. 3)	19. προλέγω : I foretell, tell in advance (v. 6)
7. ἡ πορνεία : prostitution, fornication (v. 3)	20. διαμαρτύρομαι : I testify of, bear witness to (v. 6)
8. τὸ σκεῦος : object, property; vessel (v. 4)	21. ἡ ἀκαθαρσία : refuse; immorality (v. 7)
9. κτάομαι : I get, acquire, secure; control one's own body (with σκεῦος) (v. 4)	22. τοιγαροῦν : then, therefore, for that very reason (v. 8)
10. ἡ τιμή : honor, respect (v. 4)	23. ἀθετέω : nullify, ignore; reject (v. 8)
11. τὸ πάθος : passion (v. 5)	24. ἡ φιλαδελφία : love of brother or sister (v. 9)
12. ἡ ἐπιθυμία : desire, longing; craving (v. 5)	25. ἡ χρεία : need, what should be (v. 9)
13. καθάπερ : just as (v. 5)	26. θεοδίδακτος : taught or instructed by God (v. 9)

1 Thessalonians 4:1

20. **περιπατεῖν**: Infinitive structure, infinitive usage, word related to? [1+1+1]

---

21. **ἀρέσκειν**: Infinitive structure, infinitive usage, word related to? [1+1+1]

---

1 Thessalonians 4:2

22. **γάρ**: What kind of conjunction is this? What is it referring back to? [2+2]

● 1 Thessalonians 4:3

23. γάρ: What kind of conjunction is this? What is it referring back to? [2+1]

_____

24. ἀπέχεσθαι: Infinitive structure, infinitive usage, word related to? [1+1+1]

_____

1 Thessalonians 4:4

25. εἰδέναι: Infinitive structure, infinitive usage, word related to? [1+1+1]

_____

26. σκεῦος: Read the entry in BDAG on this word. Name two interpretive options they give for its usage in this verse. [1+1]

_____

_____

27. κτᾶσθαι: Infinitive structure, infinitive usage? (This infinitive is dependent on the previous infinitive, εἰδέναι. Since εἰδέναι is a transitive verb and a verb of perception, how should you classify κτᾶσθαι?) [1+1]

_____

1 Thessalonians 4:6

28. ὑπερβαίνειν: Infinitive structure, infinitive usage, word related to? [1+1+1]

_____

29. πλεονεκτεῖν: Infinitive structure, infinitive usage, word related to? [1+1+1]

_____

1 Thessalonians 4:7

30. ἐπὶ ἀκαθαρσίᾳ ἀλλ᾽ ἐν ἁγιασμῷ: These two prepositions are set in opposition to each other, yet there seems to be an imbalance here. It is possible that ἐπί means "for" and ἐν means "in" (so ESV); or both could have the general sense of "to" (so REB). Read at least one exegetical commentary on this verse and offer an explanation for the different prepositions. [4]

_____

_____

1 Thessalonians 4:8

31. τοιγαροῦν: What type of conjunction is this? What is it referring back to? [2+2]

_____

1 Thessalonians 4:9

- γράφειν (The subject of this infinitive is implied. It is either ἡμᾶς or τινά. A paraphrastic translation thus is, "[you have no need that we should] write [to you].")

32. γράφειν: Infinitive structure, infinitive usage, word related to? [1+1+1]

_____

33. αὐτοί: Use of pronoun, word related to? [1+2]

_____

34. ἀγαπᾶν: Infinitive structure, infinitive usage, word related to? [1+1+1]

_____

Lesson 18: Participle (Part I)

Warm-Up Passage

Vocabulary

1. ὄψιος : late; evening (subst.) (v. 20)	4. σφόδρα : greatly, extremely (v. 22)
2. ἀνάκειμαι : I recline, dine (v. 20)	5. μήτι : not (v. 22)
3. λυπέω : I become sad, distressed (pass.) (v. 22)	

Matthew 26:20–22

26:20 Ὀψίας δὲ γενομένης ἀνέκειτο μετὰ τῶν δώδεκα. **26:21** καὶ ἐσθιόντων αὐτῶν εἶπεν· ἀμὴν λέγω ὑμῖν ὅτι εἷς ἐξ ὑμῶν παραδώσει με. **26:22** καὶ λυπούμενοι σφόδρα ἤρξαντο λέγειν αὐτῷ εἷς ἕκαστος· μήτι ἐγώ εἰμι, κύριε;

1. γενομένης: Mood, usage of mood, word related to? [1+2+1]

   _____

2. ἐσθιόντων: Mood, usage of mood, word related to? [1+2+1]

   _____

3. λυπούμενοι: Mood, usage of mood, word related to? [1+2+1]

   _____

Syntax Passages

Philippians 2:6–11

Background

The apostle exhorts his readers to live humbly as servants of Christ (2:1-11). He appeals to them on the basis of membership in the body of Christ (2:1-4), reminding them that selfishness hurts everyone. Then he seems to weave an early Christian hymn into the fabric of his argument. The *kenosis* (or "emptying") (2:6-11) functions as a reminder for them to follow in the steps of Christ: if he who was in the "form of God" could humble himself, what right do believers have to refrain from doing the same thing? After Christ "emptied himself" (by adding humanity, 2:6–8) God exalted him (2:9–11).

Text

2:6 ὃς ἐν μορφῇ θεοῦ ὑπάρχων
οὐχ ἁρπαγμὸν ἡγήσατο
　　τὸ εἶναι ἴσα θεῷ,
2:7 ἀλλὰ ἑαυτὸν ἐκένωσεν
　　μορφὴν δούλου λαβών,
ἐν ὁμοιώματι ἀνθρώπων γενόμενος·
　　καὶ σχήματι εὑρεθεὶς ὡς ἄνθρωπος
2:8 ἐταπείνωσεν ἑαυτὸν
γενόμενος ὑπήκοος μέχρι θανάτου,
　　θανάτου δὲ σταυροῦ.
2:9 διὸ καὶ ὁ θεὸς αὐτὸν ὑπερύψωσεν
καὶ ἐχαρίσατο αὐτῷ τὸ ὄνομα
　　τὸ ὑπὲρ πᾶν ὄνομα,
2:10 ἵνα ἐν τῷ ὀνόματι Ἰησοῦ
πᾶν γόνυ κάμψῃ
　　ἐπουρανίων καὶ ἐπιγείων καὶ καταχθονίων
2:11 καὶ πᾶσα γλῶσσα ἐξομολογήσηται ὅτι
κύριος Ἰησοῦς Χριστὸς
　　εἰς δόξαν θεοῦ πατρός.

Vocabulary

1. ἡ μορφή : form; outward appearance (v. 6)	11. ὁ σταυρός : cross (lit. and fig.) (v. 8)
2. ὁ ἁρπαγμός : something to grasp; prize (v. 6)	12. ὑπερυψόω : I raise, exalt (v. 9)
3. ἡγέομαι : I think, consider, regard (v. 6)	13. χαρίζομαι : I give graciously, grant; forgive, pardon (v. 9)
4. ἴσος : equal, same, consistent (v. 6)	14. τὸ γόνυ : knee (v. 10)
5. κενόω : I empty, divest of prestige (v. 7)	15. κάμπτω : I bend, bow (v. 10)
6. τὸ ὁμοίωμα : likeness; image, appearance (v. 7)	16. ἐπουράνιος : heavenly; heavenly things (subst.); in heaven (v. 10)
7. τὸ σχῆμα : outward appearance, form; way of life (v. 7)	17. ἐπίγειος : earthly; worldly things (subst.); on earth (v. 10)
8. ταπεινόω : I lower; humble (v. 8)	18. καταχθόνιος : under the earth, subterranean; beings under the earth (subst.) (v. 10)

9. ὑπήκοος : obedient (v. 8)	19. ἐξομολογέω : I promise; confess (mid.); acknowledge (v. 11)
10. μέχρι : until; as far as (v. 8)	

Philippians 2:6

4. ὑπάρχων: Mood, use, word related to? [1+2+1]

_____

Philippians 2:7

5. ἀλλά: This conjunction is adversative, contrasting what two elements? [4]

_____

6. λαβών: Mood, use, word related to? [1+2+1]

_____

7. γενόμενος: Mood, use, word related to? [1+2+1]

_____

8. εὑρεθείς: Mood, use, word related to? [1+2+1]

_____

Philippians 2:8

9. γενόμενος: Mood, use, word related to? [1+2+1]

_____

10. μέχρι: How does BDAG take this word? [2]

_____

Philippians 2:9

11. διό: What type of conjunction is this? What is it referring back to? [2+2]

_____

12. τό²: Function of the article? Word related to? [2+2]

_____

Philippians 2:11

13. κύριος: Case, case usage, word related to? [1+2+1]

_____

Ephesians 2:1–10

Background

Ephesians 2 addresses two issues: individual reconciliation between God and humans (2:1-10), and corporate reconciliation between Jews and Gentiles (2:11-22). In the detailing of individual reconciliation (2:1-10) there are two basic parts. First, a dark picture of believers' former state is painted: believers were controlled by Satan and destined for hell (2:1-3). Then, they were delivered from this fate: God in his mercy saved them (2:4-10). Not only did he save them, but he also proleptically caused them to reign with Christ (2:5-6). Further, they are now to be a monument to him by doing good words (2:10).

Text

2:1 Καὶ ὑμᾶς ὄντας νεκροὺς τοῖς παραπτώμασιν καὶ ταῖς ἁμαρτίαις ὑμῶν, **2:2** ἐν αἷς ποτε περιεπατήσατε κατὰ τὸν αἰῶνα τοῦ κόσμου τούτου, κατὰ τὸν ἄρχοντα τῆς ἐξουσίας τοῦ ἀέρος, τοῦ πνεύματος τοῦ νῦν ἐνεργοῦντος ἐν τοῖς υἱοῖς τῆς ἀπειθείας· **2:3** ἐν οἷς καὶ ἡμεῖς πάντες ἀνεστράφημέν ποτε ἐν ταῖς ἐπιθυμίαις τῆς σαρκὸς ἡμῶν ποιοῦντες τὰ θελήματα τῆς σαρκὸς καὶ τῶν διανοιῶν, καὶ ἤμεθα τέκνα φύσει ὀργῆς ὡς καὶ οἱ λοιποί· **2:4** ὁ δὲ θεὸς πλούσιος ὢν ἐν ἐλέει, διὰ τὴν πολλὴν ἀγάπην αὐτοῦ ἣν ἠγάπησεν ἡμᾶς, **2:5** καὶ ὄντας ἡμᾶς νεκροὺς τοῖς παραπτώμασιν συνεζωοποίησεν τῷ Χριστῷ,—χάριτί ἐστε σεσωσμένοι—**2:6** καὶ συνήγειρεν καὶ συνεκάθισεν ἐν τοῖς ἐπουρανίοις ἐν Χριστῷ Ἰησοῦ, **2:7** ἵνα ἐνδείξηται ἐν τοῖς αἰῶσιν τοῖς ἐπερχομένοις τὸ ὑπερβάλλον πλοῦτος τῆς χάριτος αὐτοῦ ἐν χρηστότητι ἐφ' ἡμᾶς ἐν Χριστῷ Ἰησοῦ. **2:8** τῇ γὰρ χάριτί ἐστε σεσωσμένοι διὰ πίστεως· καὶ τοῦτο οὐκ ἐξ ὑμῶν, θεοῦ τὸ δῶρον· **2:9** οὐκ ἐξ ἔργων, ἵνα μή τις καυχήσηται. **2:10** αὐτοῦ γάρ ἐσμεν ποίημα, κτισθέντες ἐν Χριστῷ Ἰησοῦ ἐπὶ ἔργοις ἀγαθοῖς οἷς προητοίμασεν ὁ θεός, ἵνα ἐν αὐτοῖς περιπατήσωμεν.

Vocabulary

1. τὸ παράπτωμα : offense, sin (v. 1)	15. συνεγείρω : I raise with (v. 6)
2. ποτέ : at sometime or other, formerly (v. 2)	16. συγκαθίζω : I cause to sit down with (v. 6)
3. ὁ ἄρχων : ruler; authority, leader (v. 2)	17. ἐπουράνιος : heavenly; heavenly realm (subst.) (v. 6)
4. ὁ ἀήρ : air; sky, space (v. 2)	18. ἐνδείκνυμι : I show, demonstrate (v. 7)
5. ἐνεργέω : I work, am active; produce (v. 2)	19. ἐπέρχομαι : I come, arrive (v. 7)
6. ἡ ἀπείθεια : disobedience, disbelief (v. 2)	20. ὑπερβάλλω : I go beyond, surpass (v. 7)
7. ἀναστρέφω : I act, behave, conduct oneself (v. 3)	21. ὁ, τὸ πλοῦτος : wealth; abundance (v. 7)
8. ἡ ἐπιθυμία : desire, longing; craving (v. 3)	22. ἡ χρηστότης : uprightness; goodness, kindness (v. 7)
9. ἡ διάνοια : understanding, intelligence, mind (v. 3)	23. τὸ δῶρον : gift, present, offering (v. 8)
10. ἡ φύσις : natural endowment or condition; nature (v. 3)	24. καυχάομαι : I boast, glory, pride myself, boast about (v. 9)
11. ἡ ὀργή : anger; wrath, indignation (v. 3)	25. τὸ ποίημα : work, creation (v. 10)
12. πλούσιος : rich, wealthy (v. 4)	26. κτίζω : I create, make (v. 10)
13. τὸ ἔλεος : mercy, compassion (v. 4)	27. προετοιμάζω : I prepare beforehand (v. 10)
14. συζωοποιέω : I make alive together with (v. 5)	

Ephesians 2:1

14. ὄντας: Mood, use, word related to? [1+2+1]

Ephesians 2:2

15. ἐνεργοῦντος: Mood, use, word related to? [1+2+1]

Ephesians 2:3

16. ἐν οἷς: Note that both v. 2 and v. 3 start off with a prepositional phrase with a plural relative pronoun. Name the antecedent of each below, and give a gloss for each preposition. [1+1+1+1]

_____

_____

17. ποιοῦντες: Name two possible ways to take this participle; translate the participle along with the word it depends on. [2+2]

_____

_____

Ephesians 2:4

18. ὤν: Mood, use, word related to? [1+2+2]

_____

Ephesians 2:5

19. ὄντας: Mood, use, word related to? [1+2+1]

_____

20. σεσῳσμένοι: Mood, use, word related to? [1+2+1]

_____

Ephesians 2:7

21. ἐπερχομένοις: Mood, use, word related to? [1+2+1]

_____

22. ὑπερβάλλον: Mood, use, word related to? [1+2+1]

_____

Ephesians 2:8

23. σεσῳσμένοι: Mood, use, word related to? [1+2+1]

_____

Ephesians 2:10

24. γάρ: This explanatory conjunction is looking back. State in your own words what it is explaining. [3]

_____

_____

25. κτισθέντες: Give a translation of αὐτοῦ γάρ ἐσμεν ποίημα, κτισθέντες ἐν Χριστῷ Ἰησοῦ, treating the participle as (1) adjectival (modifying the understood subject of ἐσμεν); (2) conditional; (3) antecedent; and (4) causal. Which of these categories do you think it belongs to? Why? [1+1+1+1+2]

_____

_____

_____

Lesson 19: Participle (Part II)

Warm-Up Passages

Vocabulary

1. πέμπτος : fifth (Rev 9:1)	8. εὐχαριστέω : I am thankful; I thank (Eph 1:16)
2. σαλπίζω : I blow a trumpet (Rev 9:1)	9. ἡ μνεία : mention; memory (Eph 1:16)
3. ὁ ἀστήρ : star (Rev 9:1)	10. παραιτέομαι : I make an excuse (Lk 14:18)
4. ἡ κλείς : key (Rev 9:1)	11. ὁ ἀγρός : field, farm (Lk 14:18)
5. τὸ φρέαρ : well, pit (Rev 9:1)	12. ἀγοράζω : I buy, acquire (Lk 14:18)
6. ἡ ἄβυσσος : abyss, netherworld (Rev 9:1)	13. ἡ ἀνάγκη : necessity, distress (Lk 14:18)
7. παύω : I stop; cease (mid.) (Eph 1:16)	

Revelation 9:1

Καὶ ὁ πέμπτος ἄγγελος ἐσάλπισεν· καὶ εἶδον ἀστέρα ἐκ τοῦ οὐρανοῦ πεπτωκότα εἰς τὴν γῆν, καὶ ἐδόθη αὐτῷ ἡ κλεὶς τοῦ φρέατος τῆς ἀβύσσου.

1. **πεπτωκότα**: Use of the participle, word related to? [1+1]

_____

2. **αὐτῷ**: Use of pronoun, antecedent? [1+1]

_____

Ephesians 1:16

οὐ παύομαι εὐχαριστῶν ὑπὲρ ὑμῶν μνείαν ποιούμενος ἐπὶ τῶν προσευχῶν μου.

3. **εὐχαριστῶν**: Use of the participle, word related to? [1+1]

_____

4. ποιούμενος: Use of the participle, word related to? [1+1]

_____

5. ἐπί: Use of preposition, word related to? [1+1]

_____

Luke 14:18

καὶ ἤρξαντο ἀπὸ μιᾶς πάντες παραιτεῖσθαι. ὁ πρῶτος εἶπεν αὐτῷ· ἀγρὸν ἠγόρασα καὶ ἔχω ἀνάγκην ἐξελθὼν ἰδεῖν αὐτόν· ἐρωτῶ σε, ἔχε με παρῃτημένον.

* ἀπὸ μιᾶς πάντες (This idiom means something like "all, from one [voice]"—that is, each person made similar excuses.)

6. παραιτεῖσθαι: Infinitive structure, infinitive use, word related to? [1+1+1]

_____

7. ἐξελθών: Mood, use of mood, word related to? [1+1+1]

_____

8. ἰδεῖν: Infinitive structure, infinitive use, word related to? [1+1+1]

_____

9. παρῃτημένον: Mood, use of mood, word related to? [1+1+1]

_____

Syntax Passages

Acts 13:26–31

Background

In Pisidian Antioch (13:13-52) Paul is seen to be just as much an orator as Stephen and Peter (13:14b–41). In fact, his message seems to be an amalgamation of both Stephen's speech and Peter's sermons. In vv. 23–31, Paul recounts the details of the life, death, and resurrection of Jesus Christ.

Text

13:26 Ἄνδρες ἀδελφοί, υἱοὶ γένους Ἀβραὰμ καὶ οἱ ἐν ὑμῖν φοβούμενοι τὸν θεόν, ἡμῖν ὁ λόγος τῆς σωτηρίας ταύτης ἐξαπεστάλη. **13:27** οἱ γὰρ κατοικοῦντες ἐν Ἰερουσαλήμ καὶ οἱ ἄρχοντες αὐτῶν τοῦτον ἀγνοήσαντες καὶ τὰς φωνὰς τῶν προφητῶν τὰς κατὰ πᾶν σάββατον ἀναγινωσκομένας κρίναντες ἐπλήρωσαν, **13:28** καὶ μηδεμίαν αἰτίαν θανάτου εὑρόντες ᾐτήσαντο Πιλᾶτον ἀναιρεθῆναι αὐτόν. **13:29** ὡς δὲ ἐτέλεσαν πάντα τὰ περὶ αὐτοῦ γεγραμμένα, καθελόντες ἀπὸ τοῦ ξύλου ἔθηκαν εἰς μνημεῖον. **13:30** ὁ δὲ θεὸς ἤγειρεν αὐτὸν ἐκ νεκρῶν, **13:31** ὃς ὤφθη ἐπὶ ἡμέρας πλείους τοῖς συναναβᾶσιν αὐτῷ ἀπὸ τῆς Γαλιλαίας εἰς Ἰερουσαλήμ, οἵτινες νῦν εἰσιν μάρτυρες αὐτοῦ πρὸς τὸν λαόν.

Vocabulary

1. τὸ γένος : descendant; family; nation (v. 26)	9. ἀναιρέω : I take away; kill, destroy (v. 28)
2. ἡ σωτηρία : salvation, deliverance, preservation (v. 26)	10. τελέω : finish, complete; accomplish (v. 29)
3. ἐξαποστέλλω : I send out; send away (v. 26)	11. καθαιρέω : tear down, destroy, conquer (v. 29)
4. κατοικέω : I live, dwell; inhabit (v. 27)	12. τὸ ξύλον : wood, tree (v. 29)
5. ὁ ἄρχων : ruler, lord, prince, official (v. 27)	13. τὸ μνημεῖον : monument; grave, tomb (v. 29)
6. ἀγνοέω : I do not know, do not understand (v. 27)	14. συναναβαίνω : I come or go up with (v. 31)
7. ἀναγινώσκω I read, read aloud (v. 27)	15. ὁ μάρτυς : witness, martyr (v. 31)
8. ἡ αἰτία : cause, reason (v. 28)	

Acts 13:26

10. **φοβούμενοι**: Mood, use of mood, word related to? [1+1+1]

Acts 13:27

- Verse 27 is a bit tricky to translate. The key is to understand how the participles are functioning and to have a mental diagram in view. The following may be helpful. The subject and its modifiers are: οἱ γὰρ κατοικοῦντες ἐν Ἰερουσαλήμ καὶ οἱ ἄρχοντες αὐτῶν. The main verb comes at the end of the verse: ἐπλήρωσαν. There are three participles. The first (ἀγνοήσαντες) is directly dependent on ἐπλήρωσαν. This participle takes a compound direct object: τοῦτον … καὶ τὰς φωνάς. The second object has a genitive modifier τῶν προφητῶν and an adjectival participle in second attributive position (τὰς … ἀναγινωσκομένας) with an embedded prepositional phrase (κατὰ πᾶν σάββατον). This leaves only κρίναντες to analyze. Look at the ending and think about how it is being used. You should be able to figure it out. When you read complex sentences such as this, it's best to observe carefully the inflections and think diagrammatically: What belongs on the base line? What is subordinate to it? And most important: don't panic! It takes some work, but such texts are a good challenge because they introduce you to some of the better Greek of the NT.)

11. κατοικοῦντες: Mood, use of mood, word related to? [1+1+1]

_____

12. ἀγνοήσαντες: This participle could conceivably be either attendant circumstance to ἐπλήρωσαν or causal to ἐπλήρωσαν. There is a significant difference in the resultant meaning between these two. Translate ἀγνοήσαντες … ἐπλήρωσαν both ways below. [1+1]

_____

_____

13. ἀναγινωσκομένας: Mood, use of mood, word related to? [1+1+1]

_____

14. κρίναντες: Mood, use of mood, word related to? [1+1+1]

_____

Acts 13:28

15. εὑρόντες: Mood, use of mood, word related to? [1+1+1]

_____

• ἀναιρεθῆναι (This infinitive is an example of a causative passive. With the verb ᾐτήσαντο the idea is "they asked [Pilate] to have [him] executed.")

Acts 13:29

16. γεγραμμένα: Mood, use of mood, word related to? [1+1+1]

_____

17. καθελόντες: Mood, use of mood, word related to? [1+1+1]

_____

Acts 13:31

18. συναναβᾶσιν: Mood, use of mood, word related to? [1+1+1]

_____

Acts 18:18–26

Background

After a relatively unsuccessful ministry with the philosophers in Athens, Paul traveled to Corinth (18:1–18a), where he was able to settle down for the first time because of God's protection of his ministry (18:5–11). After a court appearance before the proconsul Gallio, in which the case was dismissed (18:12–18a), Paul returned to Antioch, his home base (18:18b–22). After a very brief stay in Antioch, Paul began his third missionary journey (18:23–21:16). He had left Priscilla and Aquila, two of his coworkers, in Ephesus on his return trip to Antioch. Now he was returning to Ephesus, by way of the Galatian region (18:23). Meanwhile, Priscilla and Aquila had met Apollos in Ephesus and had given him careful instruction about the new religion (18:24–26).

Text

18:18 Ὁ δὲ Παῦλος ἔτι προσμείνας ἡμέρας ἱκανὰς τοῖς ἀδελφοῖς ἀποταξάμενος ἐξέπλει εἰς τὴν Συρίαν, καὶ σὺν αὐτῷ Πρίσκιλλα καὶ Ἀκύλας, κειράμενος ἐν Κεγχρεαῖς τὴν κεφαλήν, εἶχεν γὰρ εὐχήν. **18:19** κατήντησαν δὲ εἰς Ἔφεσον, κἀκείνους κατέλιπεν αὐτοῦ, αὐτὸς δὲ εἰσελθὼν εἰς τὴν συναγωγὴν διελέξατο τοῖς Ἰουδαίοις. **18:20** ἐρωτώντων δὲ αὐτῶν ἐπὶ πλείονα χρόνον μεῖναι οὐκ ἐπένευσεν, **18:21** ἀλλὰ ἀποταξάμενος καὶ εἰπών· πάλιν ἀνακάμψω πρὸς ὑμᾶς τοῦ θεοῦ θέλοντος, ἀνήχθη ἀπὸ τῆς Ἐφέσου, **18:22** καὶ κατελθὼν εἰς Καισάρειαν, ἀναβὰς καὶ ἀσπασάμενος τὴν ἐκκλησίαν κατέβη εἰς Ἀντιόχειαν.

18:23 καὶ ποιήσας χρόνον τινὰ ἐξῆλθεν διερχόμενος καθεξῆς τὴν Γαλατικὴν χώραν καὶ Φρυγίαν, ἐπιστηρίζων πάντας τοὺς μαθητάς.

18:24 Ἰουδαῖος δέ τις Ἀπολλῶς ὀνόματι, Ἀλεξανδρεὺς τῷ γένει, ἀνὴρ λόγιος, κατήντησεν εἰς Ἔφεσον, δυνατὸς ὢν ἐν ταῖς γραφαῖς. **18:25** οὗτος ἦν κατηχημένος τὴν ὁδὸν τοῦ κυρίου καὶ ζέων τῷ πνεύματι ἐλάλει καὶ ἐδίδασκεν ἀκριβῶς τὰ περὶ τοῦ Ἰησοῦ, ἐπιστάμενος μόνον τὸ βάπτισμα

● Ἰωάννου· **18:26** οὗτός τε ἤρξατο παρρησιάζεσθαι ἐν τῇ συναγωγῇ. ἀκούσαντες δὲ αὐτοῦ Πρίσκιλλα καὶ Ἀκύλας προσελάβοντο αὐτὸν καὶ ἀκριβέστερον αὐτῷ ἐξέθεντο τὴν ὁδὸν τοῦ θεοῦ.

Vocabulary

1. προσμένω : I remain or stay with (v. 18)	22. ἡ Ἀντιόχεια : Antioch (v. 22)
2. ἱκανός : sufficient, large, many, able, fit; bond (subst.) (v. 18)	23. διέρχομαι : I go through, cross over (v. 23)
3. ἀποτάσσω : I say farewell; give up (mid. in NT) (v. 18)	24. καθεξῆς : in orderly sequence (v. 23)
4. ἐκπλέω : I sail away (v. 18)	25. Γαλατικός : Galatian (v. 23)
5. ἡ Συρία : Syria (v. 18)	26. ἡ χώρα : land; region; country (v. 23)
6. ἡ Πρίσκιλλα : Priscilla (v. 18)	27. ἡ Φρυγία : Phrygia (v. 23)
7. ὁ Ἀκύλας : Aquila (v. 18)	28. ἐπιστηρίζω : I strengthen (v. 23)
8. κείρω : I shear; cut one's hair (v. 18)	29. ὁ Ἀπολλώς : Apollos (v. 24)
9. αἱ Κεγχρεαί : Cenchreae (v. 18)	30. ὁ Ἀλεξανδρεύς : Alexandrian (v. 24)
10. ἡ εὐχή : prayer; vow (v. 18)	31. τὸ γένος : descendant; family; nation (v. 24)
11. καταντάω : I come (to), reach; arrive at (v. 19)	32. λόγιος : learned, cultured (v. 24)
12. ἡ Ἔφεσος : Ephesus (v. 19)	33. δυνατός : powerful, strong, mighty (v. 24)
13. κἀκεῖνος : and that (one or thing), that one, or he also (v. 19)	34. κατηχέω : I inform; instruct (v. 25)
14. καταλείπω : I leave (behind) (v. 19)	35. ζέω : I am enthusiastic, excited (v. 25)
15. αὐτοῦ : here, there (v. 19)	36. ἀκριβῶς : accurately, carefully (v. 25)
16. διαλέγομαι : I converse, discuss; inform (v. 19)	37. ἐπίσταμαι : I understand; know (v. 25)
17. ἐπινεύω : I give consent (v. 20)	38. τὸ βάπτισμα : baptism (v. 25)
18. ἀνακάμπτω : I return (v. 21)	39. παρρησιάζομαι : I speak freely or fearlessly (v. 26)
19. ἀνάγω : I lead or bring up; put out to sea (v. 21)	40. προσλαμβάνω : (mid. in NT) to take (in) (v. 26)
20. κατέρχομαι : I come down; arrive (v. 22)	41. ἐκτίθημι : I expose, abandon; expound, explain (v. 26)
21. ἡ Καισάρεια : Caesarea (v. 22)	

Acts 18:18

19. προσμείνας: Mood, use of mood, word related to? [1+1+1]

_____

20. ἀποταξάμενος: Mood, use of mood, word related to? [1+1+1]

_____

- ἐξέπλει (This is an ingressive imperfect. Such imperfects are routinely used to introduce a new action in the narrative. Here the translation "set sail" seems to fit well, but the reason for the imperfect is that it gives an internal perspective, often implying that the details of what happens after the beginning of the action are yet to come. The following participle occurs within the time-frame of the imperfect. Thus, "they began sailing ... when he cut his hair [an event that occurs during the trip].")

21. κειράμενος: Mood, use of mood, word related to? [1+1+1]

_____

Acts 18:19

- αὐτοῦ (This is the neuter genitive singular of αὐτός. It functions as an adverb of place: "there.")

22. εἰσελθών: Mood, use of mood, word related to? [1+1+1]

_____

Acts 18:20

23. ἐρωτώντων: Mood, use of mood, word related to? [1+1+1]

_____

Acts 18:21

24. ἀποταξάμενος: Mood, use of mood, word related to? [1+1+1]

_____

25. εἰπών: Mood, use of mood, word related to? [1+1+1]

_____

26. θέλοντος: Mood, use of mood, word related to? [1+1+1]

_____

Acts 18:22

27. κατελθών: Mood, use of mood, word related to? [1+1+1]

_____

28. ἀναβάς: Mood, use of mood, word related to? [1+1+1]

_____

29. ἀσπασάμενος: Mood, use of mood, word related to? [1+1+1]

_____

Acts 18:23

30. ποιήσας: Mood, use of mood, word related to? [1+1+1]

_____

31. διερχόμενος: Mood, use of mood, word related to? [1+1+1]

_____

32. ἐπιστηρίζων: Mood, use of mood, word related to? [1+1+1]

_____

Acts 18:24

33. ὤν: Mood, use of mood, word related to? [1+1+1]

Acts 18:25

34. κατηχημένος: Mood, use of mood, word related to? [1+1+1]

35. ζέων: Mood, use of mood, word related to? [1+1+1]

36. ἐλάλει: Tense, tense usage? [1+1]

37. ἐδίδασκεν: Mood, use of mood, word related to? [1+1]

38. ἐπιστάμενος: Mood, use of mood, word related to? [1+1+1]

Acts 18:26

39. ἀκούσαντες: Mood, use of mood, word related to? [1+1+1]

40. ἀκριβέστερον: Use of this form of the adjective? [1]

Lesson 20: Conditional Sentences

All questions about conditional clauses, unless otherwise specified, are asking for *both* the number (first, second, third, fourth, or fifth class) and the name of the condition (first: assumed true; second: either present contrary-to-fact *or* past contrary-to-fact; third: more probable future; fourth: less probable future; fifth: present general). If the question has to do with the semantic category, consult *Basics* 304–6; *ExSyn* 682–84 for the kind of answer you should give.

Warm-Up Passages

Vocabulary

1. κολοβόω : I shorten (Mk 13:20)	11. τὰ Γόμορρα : Gomorrah (Ro 9:29)
2. ἐκλεκτός : chosen; elect; picked (Mk 13:20)	12. ὁμοιόω : I make like, compare (Ro 9:29)
3. ἐκλέγομαι : I choose; select (Mk 13:20)	13. ὁ χόρτος : grass (Mt 6:30)
4. ἴδε : look, see, behold (Mk 13:21)	14. ὁ ἀγρός : field (Mt 6:30)
5. προλέγω : I tell beforehand, in advance (Ro 9:29)	15. σήμερον : today (Mt 6:30)
6. ὁ Ἠσαΐας : Isaiah (Ro 9:29)	16. αὔριον : next day, tomorrow (Mt 6:30)
7. Σαβαώθ : Sabaoth; Lord of hosts (with κύριος) (Ro 9:29)	17. ὁ κλίβανος : oven (Mt 6:30)
8. ἐγκαταλείπω : I leave, forsake, abandon (Ro 9:29)	18. ἀμφιέννυμι : I clothe, dress (Mt 6:30)
9. τὸ σπέρμα : seed, offspring (Ro 9:29)	19. ὀλιγόπιστος : of little faith (Mt 6:30)
10. τὰ Σόδομα : Sodom (Ro 9:29)	

Mark 13:20–21

13:20 καὶ εἰ μὴ ἐκολόβωσεν κύριος τὰς ἡμέρας, οὐκ ἂν ἐσώθη πᾶσα σάρξ· ἀλλὰ διὰ τοὺς ἐκλεκτοὺς οὓς ἐξελέξατο ἐκολόβωσεν τὰς ἡμέρας. **13:21** καὶ τότε ἐάν τις ὑμῖν εἴπῃ· ἴδε ὧδε ὁ Χριστός· ἴδε ἐκεῖ, μὴ πιστεύετε.

1. εἰ: What type of conditional clause is this? What are the structural clues that tell you this? [4+4]

_____

_____

2. ἐάν: What type of conditional clause is this? What are the structural clues that indicate this? [4+4]

_____

Romans 9:29

καὶ καθὼς προείρηκεν Ἠσαΐας· εἰ μὴ κύριος σαβαὼθ ἐγκατέλιπεν ἡμῖν σπέρμα, ὡς Σόδομα ἂν ἐγενήθημεν καὶ ὡς Γόμορρα ἂν ὡμοιώθημεν.

3. εἰ: What type of conditional clause is this? What are the structural clues that tell you this? What semantic category does this belong to? [4+4+4]

_____

_____

Matthew 6:30

εἰ δὲ τὸν χόρτον τοῦ ἀγροῦ σήμερον ὄντα καὶ αὔριον εἰς κλίβανον βαλλόμενον ὁ θεὸς οὕτως ἀμφιέννυσιν, οὐ πολλῷ μᾶλλον ὑμᾶς, ὀλιγόπιστοι;

4. εἰ: What type of conditional clause is this? What semantic category does this belong to? [4+4]

_____

Syntax Passages

Luke 17:1–6

Background

The journey to Jerusalem concludes with instructions in discipleship in the light of Jesus' impending death (14:25-19:27). Here especially we see miscellaneous dominical sayings, covering such diverse topics as the cost of discipleship (14:25-35), the value Jesus places on sinners (15:1-32), a proper attitude toward money (16:1-15), a proper attitude toward the presence and coming of the kingdom (17:20-37), the necessity of reliance on God (18:15-19:10), and the like. In the passage for this lesson, Jesus instructs his disciples about stumbling blocks, forgiveness, and faith.

Text

17:1 Εἶπεν δὲ πρὸς τοὺς μαθητὰς αὐτοῦ· ἀνένδεκτόν ἐστιν τοῦ τὰ σκάνδαλα μὴ ἐλθεῖν, πλὴν οὐαὶ δι' οὗ ἔρχεται· **17:2** λυσιτελεῖ αὐτῷ εἰ λίθος μυλικὸς περίκειται περὶ τὸν τράχηλον αὐτοῦ καὶ ἔρριπται εἰς τὴν θάλασσαν ἢ ἵνα σκανδαλίσῃ τῶν μικρῶν τούτων ἕνα. **17:3** προσέχετε ἑαυτοῖς.

Ἐὰν ἁμάρτῃ ὁ ἀδελφός σου ἐπιτίμησον αὐτῷ, καὶ ἐὰν μετανοήσῃ ἄφες αὐτῷ. **17:4** καὶ ἐὰν ἑπτάκις τῆς ἡμέρας ἁμαρτήσῃ εἰς σὲ καὶ ἑπτάκις ἐπιστρέψῃ πρὸς σὲ λέγων· μετανοῶ, ἀφήσεις αὐτῷ.

17:5 Καὶ εἶπαν οἱ ἀπόστολοι τῷ κυρίῳ· πρόσθες ἡμῖν πίστιν. **17:6** εἶπεν δὲ ὁ κύριος· εἰ ἔχετε πίστιν ὡς κόκκον σινάπεως, ἐλέγετε ἂν τῇ συκαμίνῳ ταύτῃ· ἐκριζώθητι καὶ φυτεύθητι ἐν τῇ θαλάσσῃ· καὶ ὑπήκουσεν ἂν ὑμῖν.

Vocabulary

1. ἀνένδεκτος : impossible (v. 1)	13. ἁμαρτάνω : I sin (v. 3)
2. τὸ σκάνδαλον : trap; temptation (to sin) (v. 1)	14. ἐπιτιμάω : I rebuke, reprove, warn (v. 3)
3. πλήν : but, yet, however (conj.); except (impr. prep.) (v. 1)	15. μετανοέω : I repent (v. 4)
4. οὐαί : woe, alas (v. 1)	16. ἑπτάκις : seven times (v. 4)
5. λυσιτελέω : I am better; (impers.) it is better (v. 2)	17. ἐπιστρέφω : I turn around, go back (v. 4)
6. μυλικός : belonging to a mill (λίθος μυλικός : millstone [v. 2])	18. προστίθημι : I add (to), increase; grant (v. 5)
7. περίκειμαι : I am around; wear something (v. 2)	19. ὁ κόκκος : seed, grain (v. 6)
8. ὁ τράχηλος : neck, throat (v. 2)	20. τὸ σίναπι : mustard (plant) (v. 6)
9. ῥίπτω : I throw, take off (of clothing); lay down (v. 2)	21. ἡ συκάμινος : mulberry tree (v. 6)
10. σκανδαλίζω : I cause to sin; anger (v. 2)	22. ἐκριζόω : I uproot (v. 6)
11. μικρός : small, humble, short (v. 2)	23. φυτεύω : plant (v. 6)

Luke 17:1

- τοῦ τὰ σκάνδαλα μὴ ἐλθεῖν (The genitive article belongs with the infinitive; the accusative τὰ σκάνδαλα is functioning as the subject of the infinitive.)

Luke 17:2

5. εἰ: What type of conditional clause is this? What is the main verb(s) in the apodosis? [4+4]

_____

Luke 17:3

6. ἐάν[1]: What type of conditional clause is this? What are the structural clues that indicate this? [4+4]

_____

7. ἐάν[2]: What type of conditional clause is this? [4]

_____

Luke 17:4

8. ἐάν: What type of conditional clause is this? [4]

_____

9. ἀφήσεις: Tense, use of tense? [4+4]

_____

Luke 17:6

10. εἰ: What type of conditional clause is this? [4]

_____

John 8:34-42

Background

The emphasis of Jesus' instruction in this section of John is on a defense that he is from God (7:15-36) and that he is, in fact, God's Son (8:12-59).

Text

8:34 ἀπεκρίθη αὐτοῖς ὁ Ἰησοῦς· ἀμὴν ἀμὴν λέγω ὑμῖν ὅτι πᾶς ὁ ποιῶν τὴν ἁμαρτίαν δοῦλός ἐστιν τῆς ἁμαρτίας. **8:35** ὁ δὲ δοῦλος οὐ μένει ἐν τῇ οἰκίᾳ εἰς τὸν αἰῶνα, ὁ υἱὸς μένει εἰς τὸν αἰῶνα. **8:36** ἐὰν οὖν ὁ υἱὸς ὑμᾶς ἐλευθερώσῃ, ὄντως ἐλεύθεροι ἔσεσθε.

8:37 Οἶδα ὅτι σπέρμα Ἀβραάμ ἐστε· ἀλλὰ ζητεῖτέ με ἀποκτεῖναι, ὅτι ὁ λόγος ὁ ἐμὸς οὐ χωρεῖ ἐν ὑμῖν. **8:38** ἃ ἐγὼ ἑώρακα παρὰ τῷ πατρὶ λαλῶ· καὶ ὑμεῖς οὖν ἃ ἠκούσατε παρὰ τοῦ πατρὸς ποιεῖτε. **8:39** Ἀπεκρίθησαν καὶ εἶπαν αὐτῷ· ὁ πατὴρ ἡμῶν Ἀβραάμ ἐστιν. λέγει αὐτοῖς ὁ Ἰησοῦς· εἰ τέκνα τοῦ Ἀβραάμ ἐστε, τὰ ἔργα τοῦ Ἀβραὰμ ἐποιεῖτε· **8:40** νῦν δὲ ζητεῖτέ με ἀποκτεῖναι ἄνθρωπον ὃς τὴν ἀλήθειαν ὑμῖν λελάληκα ἣν ἤκουσα παρὰ τοῦ θεοῦ· τοῦτο Ἀβραὰμ οὐκ ἐποίησεν. **8:41** ὑμεῖς ποιεῖτε τὰ ἔργα τοῦ πατρὸς ὑμῶν. εἶπαν οὖν αὐτῷ· ἡμεῖς ἐκ πορνείας οὐ γεγεννήμεθα, ἕνα πατέρα ἔχομεν τὸν θεόν. **8:42** εἶπεν αὐτοῖς ὁ Ἰησοῦς· εἰ ὁ θεὸς πατὴρ ὑμῶν ἦν ἠγαπᾶτε ἂν ἐμέ, ἐγὼ γὰρ ἐκ τοῦ θεοῦ ἐξῆλθον καὶ ἥκω· οὐδὲ γὰρ ἀπ' ἐμαυτοῦ ἐλήλυθα, ἀλλ' ἐκεῖνός με ἀπέστειλεν.

Vocabulary

1. ἐλευθερόω : I free, set free (v. 36)	5. χωρέω : I go; go forward; comprehend (v. 37)
2. ὄντως : really, certainly, in truth (v. 36)	6. ἡ πορνεία : prostitution, fornication (v. 41)
3. ἐλεύθερος : free; independent (v. 36)	7. ἥκω : I have come, am present (v. 42)
4. τὸ σπέρμα : seed; descendants (v. 37)	8. ἐμαυτοῦ : (of) myself (v. 42)

John 8:36

11. ἐάν: What type of conditional clause is this? What semantic category does this belong to? [4+4]

John 8:38

- τῷ πατρί (There is no possessive pronoun with πατρί, but the article implies "my," as is obvious from the first person verbs. In light of this, how should τοῦ πατρός be understood?)

John 8:39

12. εἰ: What type of conditional clause is this? What semantic category does this belong to? [4+4]

_____

John 8:42

13. εἰ: What type of conditional clause is this? How do you know? What semantic category does this belong to? [4+4+4]

_____

Greek Grammar Beyond the Basics

An Exegetical Syntax of the New Testament

Daniel B. Wallace

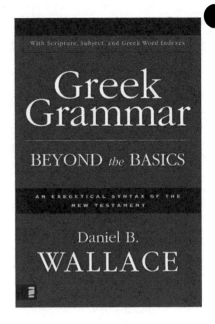

For seminary students, the goal of studying Greek grammar is the accurate exegesis of biblical texts. Sound exegesis requires that the exegete consider grammar within a larger framework that includes context, lexeme, and other linguistic features.

While the trend of some grammarians has been to take a purely grammatical approach to the language, *Greek Grammar Beyond the Basics* integrates the technical requirements for proper Greek interpretation with the actual interests and needs of Bible students. It is the first textbook to systematically link syntax and exegesis of the New Testament for second-year Greek students. It explores numerous syntactical categories, some of which have not previously been dealt with in print.

Greek Grammar Beyond the Basics is the most up-to-date Greek grammar available. It equips intermediate Greek students with the skills they need to do exegesis of biblical texts in a way that is faithful to their intended meaning. The book contains a textual index, a subject index, and a Greek word index. It closes with a Syntax Summary section.

Available in stores and online!

The Basics of New Testament Syntax

An Intermediate Greek Grammar

Daniel B. Wallace

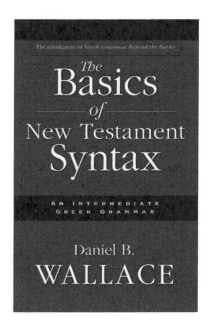

The Basics of New Testament Syntax provides concise, up-to-date guidance for intermediate Greek students to do accurate exegesis of biblical texts. Abridged from *Greek Grammar Beyond the Basics: An Exegetical Syntax of the New Testament*, the popular exegetical Greek grammar for studies in Greek by Daniel B. Wallace, *The Basics of New Testament Syntax* offers a practical grammar for second-year students.

The strengths of this abridgment will become quickly apparent to the user:

- It shows the relevance of syntax for exegesis and is thoroughly cross-referenced to *Exegetical Syntax.*
- It includes an exceptional number of categories useful for intermediate Greek studies.
- It is easy to use. Each semantic category is discussed, and a definition and key to identification are provided.
- Scores of charts and tables enable the intermediate student to grasp the material quickly.

We want to hear from you. Please send your comments about this book to us in care of zreview@zondervan.com. Thank you.

ZONDERVAN.com/
AUTHORTRACKER
follow your favorite authors